Access to His

General Editor: Keit

China: From Empire to People's Republic, 1900-49

Michael Lynch

Hodder & Stoughton

A MEMBER OF THE HODDER HEADLINE GROUP

The cover illustration is a painting of Mao speaking to the troops on the Long March, courtesy of the David King Collection.

Some other titles in the series:

The People's Republic of China
Michael Lynch

ISBN 0 340 68853 X

Stalin and Khrushchev: The USSR 1924-64
Michael Lynch

ISBN 0 340 53335 8

Stagnation and Reform: The USSR 1964-91
John Laver

ISBN 0 340 66413 4

War and Peace: International Relations 1914-45
David Williamson

ISBN 0 340 57165 9

France 1914-69: The Three Republics
Peter Neville

ISBN 0 340 56561 6

British Library Cataloguing in Publication Data

A catalogue for this title is available from the British Library

ISBN 0-340-62702-6

First published 1996

Impression number   10 9 8 7 6 5 4 3 2 1
Year   1999   1998   1997   1996

Typeset by Sempringham publishing services, Bedford
Printed in Great Britain for Hodder & Stoughton Educational,
a division of Hodder Headline Plc, 338 Euston Road, London NW1 3BH
by Redwood Books, Trowbridge, Wiltshire

growing demands for further concessions.

c) Yuan Shikai and the Regency

In November 1908 the plight of the Manchu dynasty deepened suddenly and dramatically with the death within twenty-four hours of both Emperor Guangxu and Cixi. This left the dynasty in the hands of the two-year-old Pu Yi, with the deceased Emperor's brother, Prince Chun, acting as Regent. The moment appeared to have arrived for all those who for personal or political motives wished to see the imperial system enfeebled, if not destroyed. Nevertheless, the new Regent endeavoured to preserve the royal house by continuing with the reforms that Cixi had sanctioned. In an attempted show of strength, Prince Chun dismissed from office General Yuan Shikai, the commander of the Beijing army. Yuan might best be described as an over-mighty subject. He had used his military position to become a political threat to the Manchu government. On the pretext that Yuan's war-wounds, in particular his gammy leg, made him an undignified presence at court, the Regent instructed him to take early retirement. The order, which was deliberately worded so as to make Yuan appear ridiculous, was meant to pay him back for an earlier act of disloyalty to the previous Emperor. Yuan hobbled off, vowing retribution.

The Regent had intended his actions as a sign of authority, but to opponents of the imperial system the absurd episode was simply added proof of how much of an anachronism the royal court had become. It was one thing for the government to dismiss a difficult individual, it was another for it to deal effectively with the growing opposition of whole groups of disaffected Chinese. Reforms which did not go far enough politically or economically, and yet which at the same time increased the burden of taxation, frustrated the entrepreneurial business classes. The large number of tax revolts in China during the first decade of the century was an indicator of the widespread resentment felt towards government policies.

An issue that particularly intensified anti-Manchu feelings was that of the railways. Between 1895 and 1911 there had been a boom in railway construction in China. This had stimulated considerable international investment in a number of provinces. Fearful that it would lose control of the nation's main communication system, the Beijing government announced the nationalisation of the major rail lines; owners would be compensated but not to the full value of their holdings. To pay for the nationalisation programme the government negotiated a large foreign loan. Thus to the scandal of displaced owners and cheated share-holders was added the humiliation of further indebtedness and dependency on Western bankers. The disaffected commercial lobby now played their part in organising open opposition to a government that appeared to be willing to sacrifice China's economic interests.

d) The 1911 Revolution

Such was the lack of support for the Manchu government that the last years of its life between 1908 and 1911 may be fairly described as a revolution waiting to happen. All that was needed was a spark. This was provided on 10 October 1911, known in China as the Double Tenth. On that date at Wuhan (Wuchang), a city on the River Yangzi (Yangtze) in Hubei (Hupei) province, troops refused to obey an order to suppress a group of dissidents. The incident was of no great moment in itself; local difficulties of this kind had been frequent in recent Chinese history. However, in the charged circumstances of the time, military insubordination took on an added significance. A rash of similar mutinies occurred in neighbouring provinces. Seizing the moment, local political revolutionaries joined with the military in defiance of Beijing. By the end of November, all but three of China's provinces south of Beijing had declared themselves independent of central government control. Events took a further revolutionary turn in November when delegates from the rebellious provinces gathered in Nanjing (Nanking) to declare the establishment of a Chinese republic. Sun Yatsen, who was in the USA and had therefore played no direct part in the events surrounding the Double Tenth, was invited to be the Republic's first president. He returned to China and was installed as President on 1 January 1912.

What was needed if central government authority was to be reasserted was a swift and resolute response. But to achieve this Beijing would have to call on loyal commanders in the provinces, and these were hard to find. The Manchu government had lost military control of the localities. That left only one recourse, to dispatch the Beijing army southwards to reimpose the regime's authority.

So, confronted by insurrection and mutiny, the beleaguered Manchu government was obliged to appeal to the discredited Yuan Shikai to act as their saviour. Yuan expressed a willingness to do so, but only on his terms. He marched south, easily retaking a number of rebellious regions, but when his army reached Wuhan, the site of the Double Tenth, Yuan deliberately held back from seizing it. His aim was to come to terms with the revolutionaries. It was a matter of personal ambition; Yuan was far from being a political radical but he had no respect for the court which had humiliated him. He saw in the situation an opportunity to use his military strength to act as arbiter, thus leaving himself in a position of power whatever the turn of political events. The *quid pro quo* he offered the republicans was that if they would accept him in place of Sun Yatsen as president he would use his authority to establish a workable constitution and persuade the Manchus to abdicate without further resistance. No clear account of the negotiations between Yuan and the revolutionaries has survived, but it would seem that there were misgivings on both sides. However, once Sun Yatsen had expressed his willingness early in February 1912 to give way to Yuan as president, the deal was struck. Yuan then presented what amounted to an ultimatum to the Manchus - abdicate or be overthrown by force. There were hawks among the courtiers who urged that the dynasty should at least go down fighting, but the Regent and Longyu, the Dowager Empress, refused to contemplate further bloodshed. On 12 February 1912 Longyu issued a formal abdication decree on behalf of the five-year-old Emperor Pu Yi.

1 By observing the nature of the people's aspirations we learn the will of heaven ... I have induced the Emperor to yield his authority to the country as a whole, determining that there should be a constitutional republic. Yuan Shikai has full powers to organise a
5 provisional republican government to treat with the people's forces on the methods of achieving unity so that five races, Manchus, Mongols, Chinese, Muslims and Tibetans may continue together in one Chinese Republic with unimpaired territory.

The revolution of 1911-12 was a very Chinese affair. The official statement of abdication declared that the mandate of heaven had passed from the Manchus to the new Republic. The imperial family was granted a subsidy and allowed to remain living in the Forbidden City in Beijing. 1911 was only a partial revolution. What failed to emerge from it was participatory politics in anything approaching a Western sense. A number of democratic trappings appeared but the representative principle was never genuinely adopted. A clean break with the past had not been made. Many of the imperial officials continued to hold their posts, and corruption and factionalism remained the dominant features of Chinese public life.

Efforts have often been made to depict 1911 as a bourgeois revolution, but while China's middle classes may have subsequently benefited from the fall of the Qing dynasty there is little evidence that it was they who initiated the Wuhan rising. That was essentially the work of the military. It is true that the radicals then took the opportunity to join in but it was on the terms dictated by the military, who remained largely in control of things. A more convincing interpretation of the events of 1911 is to see them as a revolution of the provinces against the centre. The Double Tenth was a triumph of regionalism. It represented a particular phase in the long-running contest between central autocracy and local autonomy, a contest that was to shape much of China's history during the following forty years.

2 The Early Republic, 1912-16

The regionalism that had played such a prominent part in the 1911 revolution continued to be an influential factor in the early days of the republic. Sun Yatsen's Alliance League, which soon after the fall of the

Manchus declared itself to be a parliamentary party and adopted the name Guomindang (GMD), had offered Yuan Shikai the presidency in February in the expectation that he would come south to Nanjing to set up the new government. Their reasoning was that once he was away from his power base in Beijing it would be much easier to control him and oblige him to honour his commitment to the Republic. It was precisely for that reason that Yuan was determined to stay put. His authority was in the north and he was not prepared to weaken it by an ill-judged move. A Nanjing delegation sent to Beijing to provide him with a presidential escort for his journey south had to return without him.

The plain fact was that Sun Yatsen's republicans had been outmanoeuvred. They could, of course, have refused to recognise Yuan's presidency. But this would have been no more than a gesture. Such influence as the GMD had at this stage was restricted to the southern provinces. Whatever their claims to be a national party, they were a regional influence only. Moreover, unused to open political activity, they continued to operate as the secret-society triad that they had been before the revolution. As Sun Yatsen and some of his more astute supporters acknowledged, the GMD's naivety and lack of experience of democratic politics restricted them to a minor role in the early years of the Republic.

This was evident in the way Yuan overcame criticism and resistance from the GMD. A striking example occurred in 1913. Yuan, desperate for means to finance his government, negotiated a £25 million foreign loan. The terms imposed by the six-nation consortium that advanced the money were severely restrictive and involved the pledging of large portions of China's internal revenue as security. Republicans bitterly condemned Yuan for being as guilty of abandoning China's sovereignty as the Manchus had been. (The same charge was to be levelled against him in 1915 when he appeared supinely to give in to Japan's notorious 21 Demands.) In an attempted 'Second Revolution' the GMD tried to organise armed resistance in a number of the southern provinces. But Yuan rode the storm. Ignoring the GMD's impeachment of him for exceeding his presidential powers, Yuan either dismissed the military commanders in the key provinces or bribed them into staying loyal to him. Yuan's army then rapidly crushed such resistance as remained. It was clear that the republican parties in China were too ill-organised to mount an effective opposition. Sun Yatsen fled to Japan in November 1913, disappointed but not altogether surprised by the failure of the Second Revolution. He explained the ineffectual showing of the GMD by reference to its structure; unless the GMD reorganised itself as a disciplined, centrally directed, body it would be unable to exercise real power in China. It was in Japan that Sun Yatsen now began restructuring his party along these lines.

But, for the moment, Yuan Shikai appeared to be in control in China.

Having overcome the resistance in the provinces, he sought to consolidate his authority by permanently suspending parliament and proscribing a number of parties, including the GMD. He took a further step towards centralising his power by abolishing the regional assemblies, which had been created under the Manchus and enshrined in the 1912 republican constitution. Central control of tax revenues was imposed and local civilian administrators were made directly answerable to Beijing. Such measures were bound to excite further provincial opposition. Despite Yuan's success hitherto in imposing himself on republican China, there was a limit to the number of times he could enforce his will. His strength was relative. He was certainly more powerful than any single group or interest, but his authority was never absolute. It may well have been his awareness of this that pushed him towards the idea of resurrecting the monarchy. If he were to become emperor, he would command a degree of obedience that he could not hope to obtain merely as president. In response to what he claimed to be a spontaneous appeal from the people, but which in fact had been organised by his supporters at his behest, Yuan announced late in 1915 that for the sake of the nation he would restore the imperial title and accept it for himself. On New Year's Day 1916 he was ceremonially enthroned as Emperor.

It was a hollow triumph. Rather than unite the nation and make his rule more acceptable, his elevation aroused fiercer and more determined opposition. A succession of provinces declared their independence from Beijing and rose in revolt. More serious still was the defection of the generals in Yuan's Beijing army. For some time they had been increasingly resentful of Yuan's dictatorial and dismissive treatment of them and they informed him they would not serve him as Emperor. No commander can survive without the loyalty of his officers. Seeing the writing on the wall, Yuan renounced the throne in March 1916. Three months later he was dead.

Yuan Shikai should not be dismissed simply as a self-seeking opportunist who subordinated China's needs to his own wish for power. Modern historians, while accepting that he was motivated by personal ambition, point out that he did attempt to respond to China's most pressing needs. Despite being eventually overwhelmed by the problems he faced, Yuan's attempts at administrative and economic reform had merit. Arguably, his struggle to impose himself on the localities was a recognition on his part of a vital fact - that unless there was an effective restoration of strong central authority, China stood little chance of developing the cohesion that would enable it to grow into a modern nation state. One historian aptly refers to Yuan as a 'modernising conservative'. There is also the consideration that if Yuan Shikai had his faults then so, too, did his republican contemporaries. None of the individuals or parties involved in the early Republic had any real answers to China's constitutional and political problems. The Republic that replaced the Manchus was not well served by the mixture of naivety and corruption that passed for politics in that period.

3 The Warlord Era, 1916-27

Whatever Yuan Shikai's failings may have been, he had represented some degree of authority and order. With his passing there was no individual or party capable of preventing China from sliding into further confusion and fragmentation. Nominally, the republican government continued to function in Beijing but it exercised little real power. It was split between rival factions, the most prominent being the Anhui, the Fengtien, and the Chihli groups. Although they styled themselves parties, none of them represented a clearly defined principle or programme. Save in their personnel and their geographical location they were barely distinguishable from each other. They were no more than cliques bidding for power.

The weakness of the republican government was most evident in its inability to maintain a loyal army. This in turn meant that there was no force strong enough to impose the government's will on the provinces. It became impossible to sustain civilian government in these areas. As a direct consequence, the local regions fell under the domination of what

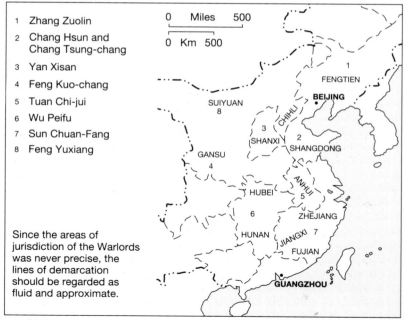

1   Zhang Zuolin
2   Chang Hsun and Chang Tsung-chang
3   Yan Xisan
4   Feng Kuo-chang
5   Tuan Chi-jui
6   Wu Peifu
7   Sun Chuan-Fang
8   Feng Yuxiang

Since the areas of jurisdiction of the Warlords was never precise, the lines of demarcation should be regarded as fluid and approximate.

Principal warlords and their areas of authority before 1926

were in effect a series of private armies, whose commanders-in-chief took over the reins of civil as well as military authority. The power of the sword predominated. The military commanders, or 'warlords' as they became known, were answerable only to themselves. They created their own laws, issued their own currency and imposed their own taxation systems. In describing the weakness of central authority against the strength of local elites, historians have likened warlord China to England during the Wars of the Roses and to Renaissance Italy in the time of the city states.

Two broad phases are identifiable in the warlord period, pre-1920 and post-1920. The first set of warlords achieved their position largely by default; that is to say, they happened to be holding provincial military governorships at the time the central authority of the republican government in Beijing began to break down. They tended to be strongly conservative in outlook. Although there was continuity after 1920, many warlords holding power well into the 1920s and beyond, there was also a tendency after that date for new military commanders to appear who did not owe their positions to previous republican appointment. They were opportunists who seized power knowing that the central government was incapable of stopping them.

Because of the common military features of their rule, it has been customary to group the warlords together as a single phenomenon, but in reality they represented a wide variety of attitudes and aspirations. The following examples suggest how different the warlords were from each other. Duan Qirui (Tuan Chi-jui), who became warlord in Anhui in 1916, had been Minister for War under Yuan Shikai. He proclaimed a strong belief in Confucian values and had gained a significant personal following, known as the 'Anfu Club', in the republican parliament. Feng Kuo-chang, who took control of Gansu (Kansu) in 1916, had also been one of Yuan's lieutenants and had played a central role in the 1911 rebellion against the Manchus; he had subsequently risen to become Vice-president of the Republic. In marked contrast was Zhang Xun (Chang Hsun), whose base was in Shandong (Shantung) province. He was a staunch supporter of the Manchu dynasty and was styled 'the pigtailed general' because he continued to wear the queue as a mark of his belief in traditional Manchu forms. In 1917 Zhang made an unsuccessful attempt to restore Pu Yi to the imperial throne.

Among the warlords who took power after 1920 was Feng Yuxiang (Feng Yu-hsiang), the 'Christian general', who baptised his troops *en masse* with a hosepipe. Feng rose from an illiterate peasant background in Suiyuan to become a self-taught upholder of a bizarre synthesis of Confucian, Christian and Buddhist teachings. He would not tolerate 'immoral' behaviour by his troops and made them sing improving hymns in place of the foul ditties they were accustomed to bawl when marching. A strikingly individual feature of Feng's rule was his conviction that the province should be governed by moral values. As totally different from Feng as it was possible to be was Zhang Zongzhang (Chang Tsung-chang), another of the warlords who emerged after 1922. Zhang was a depraved bandit who fought his way to power in Shandong province by 'splitting melons', his jolly euphemism for smashing open his opponents' heads. He took a pathological delight in terrorising the population and destroying the resources of the province.

Whatever their separate aims and individual quirks, the warlords retained one common characteristic. None of them was willing to give up his private army or submit to outside authority. As long as their rule obtained, China would stay divided. Moreover, notwithstanding the rare warlord who had genuine concern for the people of the region over which he held sway, the prevailing Chinese perception of warlord rule was one of oppression and terror.

1 Poor people of Sichuan, for ten years now we have suffered the scourge of militarism, more destructive than the floods, more destructive than savage beasts. Will it continue until not a single man, not a single hut remains in this wretched land? Ah! these 5 military governors and their officers! ... We must have soldiers, people say, so that the country will be strong. We must have armies

Feng Yuxiang, Chiang Kaishek and Yan Xishan

to protect ourselves from foreigners. And the armies are
continually recruiting men. And the people become poorer and
poorer! ... where an army has passed, nothing grows but brambles.
10 This is the case with us, where armies pass through again and
again. Our situation has become intolerable.

China's weakness during the warlord era was a commentary on the
failure of the Republic to replace Manchu autocracy with effective
central government. Regional ties had proved too strong. The belief that
the 1911 revolution would lead to the introduction of representative
government in China, had turned out to be a false one. The roots of
democracy were too shallow for it to take hold. This opened the way for
locally powerful individuals to take over the regions. It is true that there
was still a strong residual nationalism among the Chinese, which
sporadically expressed itself in passionate anti-foreigner demonstrations, but as yet it lacked a clear political focus or direction. Rather
than create political stability, the Republic had produced a political
vacuum. It thus became the goal of the two leading revolutionary
parties, the Guomindang and the Chinese Communist Party, which was
formed in 1921, to fill that void. In their early development what gave
both parties appeal and purpose was not so much what they were for but
what they were against. Although their ultimate objectives for China
might differ, they shared the basic view that an essential first step was the
removal of the two evils that characterised the warlord period,
warlordism itself and the continued subjection of China to foreign
imperialists.

The anomaly was that while the political leaders professed a deep
animosity towards the foreigners they were not above receiving
hand-outs or protection from them when in need. Sun Yatsen frequently
sought help from Japan and took sanctuary in the foreign legations. His
attempt to set up a rival Nationalist government in Guangzhou in
opposition to Beijing only added to China's divisions. Neither the
Republican government in the north nor the Nationalist one in the south
could operate independently of the warlords in those regions. Both
governments negotiated with local warlords and were quite prepared to
enlist their military support in order to sustain their own authority. The
strength of Zhang Zuolin (Chang Tso-lin), warlord in the Beijing area,
was such that a number of foreign countries chose to deal with him
rather than the official republican government in Beijing. Similarly, the
power of Wu Peifu in central China made him independent of the rival
government in Guangzhou.

Nevertheless, there were some positive features to the warlord era.
Advances were made on the economic front; some of the warlords had
progressive ideas regarding agriculture and industry. Zhang Zuolin
adopted an industrial development programme with the specific
intention of preventing a Japanese economic takeover of Manchuria.

Yan Xishan (Yen Hsi-shan), one of the longest-surviving warlords, maintained his control of the Shanxi (Shansi) region from the first year of the Republic in 1912 until the defeat of the Nationalists in 1949. During that time he introduced industrial training schemes and endeavoured to improve the quality and range of local services in the province.

Moreover, the warlord period was important for the reaction it produced. The disunity and distress that characterised the time intensified nationalist feelings in China. This produced a solidarity among Chinese radicals and gave direction and purpose to a revolutionary movement that otherwise might have continued to dissipate itself in factionalism and local rivalries. It was no accident that China's literary and intellectual renaissance reached its high point in the 1920s - the worst years of warlord rule. The humiliation of the nation at the hands of warlords and foreigners gave the Chinese a common sense of grievance. It was this that eventually checked the centripetal tendencies in republican China by providing a cause around which the Chinese could unite. Ultimately the two major revolutionary parties would engage in a long and violent struggle for supremacy, but in their initial relations what united them was greater than what divided them.

a) The 4 May Movement, 1919-25

The '4 May Movement' refers to the sustained feeling of resentment against Japan in particular and the imperialist occupiers in general. This reaction was most notable among China's intellectuals, who, disillusioned by the failure of the 1911 revolution and the Republic to achieve real advances for the country, were further dismayed by the apparent refusal of the West to extend the principles of democracy and self-determination to China. The 4 May Movement was of central importance in Chinese politics between 1919 and 1927 and played its part in preparing the ground for the reorganisation of the GMD in 1919 and the creation of the CCP in 1921. It took its name from the first day of the violent demonstration in Beijing, which followed the news of China's humiliation at the Paris Peace Conference of 1919. In April the victorious Allies, gathered at Versailles, dismissively informed the Chinese delegation that Germany's concessionary rights in Shandong province were not to be returned to China but were to be transferred instead to Japan. This was a direct reneging on the earlier promise made to China by the Allies. Indeed, it had been that commitment that had finally persuaded China at considerable cost to itself to enter the First World War on the Allied side in 1917.

How intense the Chinese sense of nationalism could be when outraged had been shown in 1915 in the disturbances that had followed Yuan Shikai's acceptance of Japan's 21 Demands. China's major cities now experienced the same reaction. In May 1919, Chinese protesters took to the streets, intent on venting their anger. Government ministers were physically attacked, and anti-Japanese boycotts were organised in Beijing and Shanghai. A Western observer described the turmoil in the capital:

1 All the educational institutions struck, formed processions and marched around the city. They intended to hold a mass meeting in the Central Park, but the police and military drove them back and made numerous arrests. This was the greatest mistake the
5 government could have made, for if the students had been allowed to hold the meeting they would not have had the opportunity of making themselves martyrs.
   During the next few days excited students could be seen in small parties in every street, working themselves into a state of delirium
10 by telling the passers-by of the indignities being thrust upon them through the fault of the pro-Japanese members of the Cabinet, whom they rightly stated were nothing more than the paid agents of Japan.
   This movement is the strongest move of its kind that the
15 Chinese have made. Not only has it spread all over China, but in Australia, Singapore, Hongkong, Vladivostok, and even as far as America. Already it has caused great alarm in Japan. This boycott is different to all others. On previous occasions it has been the Chinese merchants who have been the mainstay of such attempts,
20 but this time it is the consumer who is carrying it on. The students not only shamed the people into a refusal to purchase Japanese goods, but each one of them took a certain part of a street and explained why they should not ... Millions of dollars have been collected to start making articles which have heretofore been
25 purchased from Japan. It will not surprise me if this boycott within the next eighteen months does not cost the Japanese four hundred million dollars.

The most significant aspect of all this was the response of Chinese students and intellectuals. The radical thinkers in the universities turned even more eagerly to revolutionary theory to justify their resistance. In the excited atmosphere, the Marxist creed of violent revolution took on an added attraction and relevance. The seizure of power in Russia by the Bolsheviks in 1917 had provided a practical example of a successful popular rising against a defunct ruling class. Morover, the Bolsheviks had declared to the world that they were adopting a policy of 'peace without annexations', involving the abandonment of any claims to territories beyond Russia's borders. Here before the eyes of the Chinese revolutionaries was a Marxist government which had forsworn the old imperialism which lay at the root of China's present humiliation. It is easy to understand why Marxism captivated Chinese radicals.

Communist cells soon established themselves in the major Chinese cities, and in 1921 some twenty revolutionaries met in Shanghai to found the Chinese Communist Party. Among them was a young librarian called Mao Zedong, who was soon to became prominent as party organiser in Hunan province.

What the 4 May Movement did in the 1920s was to give a sense of direction to radicals and revolutionaries who looked to the ejection of the foreigner as a necessary stage in China's regeneration. Anti-Western and anti-Japanese demonstrations continued to occur throughout the early 1920s. The authorities managed to contain the unrest but it provided fertile opportunities for radicals to spread their propaganda. The CCP and GMD, sometimes acting together, were invariably involved in the organisation or exploitation of the protests.

b) The United Front and the Northern Expedition, 1923-7

Since its reformation in 1912 the GMD had undergone a number of internal disputes over policy, but it had remained loyal to two essentials: the leadership of Sun Yatsen, and 'the 3 Principles of the People' as its basic political programme. The third of these principles, 'the people's livelihood', was often referred to as socialism. Even though this term lacked a precise definition in its Chinese context, it convinced the Comintern that the GMD merited being considered a truly revolutionary party with which the young CCP must co-operate. The result was that by 1923 the two parties had come together under Comintern instructions to form the United Front. There were sceptics in both parties who were suspicious of the other side and doubted that the alliance could survive, but in the short term the affinity between the CCP and the GMD over the need to destroy the warlords and drive out the foreigners held the Front together.

The argument for the existence of the Front was given increased validity by the incident in 1925, which may be regarded as marking the climax of the 4 May Movement. In Shanghai on 30 May, a large crowd marched in protest against an earlier shooting of Chinese workers by Japanese factory guards. Frightened by the scale of the march, the British commander of the international settlement in the city ordered his forces to disperse the protesters with rifle fire, an overreaction that resulted in twelve deaths. The revolutionary parties immediately exploited the ensuing outrage among the Chinese to organise further strikes and riots. Attacks were made on foreign legations amid scenes reminiscent of the Boxer Rising. For days Guangzhou and Shanghai became impossible to govern. An uneasy peace was eventually restored but the incident had revealed how intense anti-foreigner sentiments had become.

For Chinese revolutionaries the 30 May affair re-emphasised the need for military strength; the internal and external enemies of China's

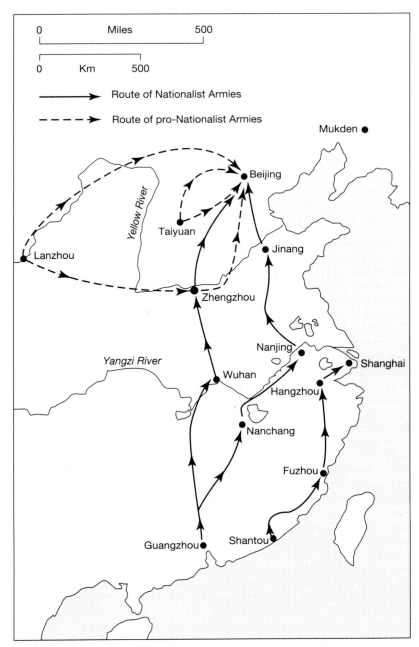

The Northern Expedition 1926-8

revolutionary progress could not be overcome except by force. This was a truth which all realists accepted. The chief beneficiary from this stress upon the role of the military was Chiang Kaishek, who shortly before the 30 May incident had become the leader of the Nationalists. In 1924 he had been appointed Commander-in-Chief at the Whampoa Military Academy at Guangzhou, the GMD's military headquarters. Chiang had used his leadership of the National Revolutionary Army, which that position gave him, to overcome his rivals within the GMD in the succession struggle that followed the death of Sun Yatsen in March 1925.

Sun Yatsen's passing was a significant moment in Chinese politics. It had the effect of releasing the anti-Communist elements within the GMD which Sun had held in check. Chiang Kaishek's success in the GMD power struggle was a victory for the military wing, the element that had close relations with the Chinese middle class and which was opposed to the social revolutionary policies of the CCP. Chiang had not shared his predecessor's belief that the CCP could be easily absorbed into the GMD and then rendered impotent. Although Chiang, along with nearly all the leading members of the GMD, had received training in Moscow in the early 1920s, he had acquired no love for Marxism. His conviction was that the Communists represented an internal challenge that had to be crushed. Chiang's determination to purge his party of Communism was soon evident. During 1926 he dismissed a number of CCP officials from their posts in the Guomindang, arrested several Comintern advisers, and pushed out of office his closest rival, Wang Jingwei (Wang Ching-wei), who had been on the left of the GMD and a civilian. This reinforced Chiang Kaishek's military control of the GMD.

However, Chiang knew that the Communists were not the only obstacle. Before he and his Nationalists could take full power in China, the warlords, who still controlled large areas of central and northern China, had to be broken. The time was ripe; the 30 May incident in 1925 had created a mood of national anger that could now be turned against warlordism. Chiang planned to combine his two objectives, the destruction of the warlords and the annihilation of the Communists, into one major campaign - the Northern Expedition. He could not, of course, openly declare his second objective until he had achieved the first. Until the warlords were defeated the GMD-CCP Front had to be preserved; he still needed the CCP and the Comintern as military allies.

The Northern Expedition proved a remarkable success. Within the two years 1926-8 the forces of the United Front had effectively broken the power of the warlords in the key provinces of eastern and central China. When Zhang Zuolin, the warlord who had controlled the Beijing area, was finally driven out in 1928, the GMD announced that it was now the legitimate government of China and that it would rule from the new capital of Nanjing.

c) The White Terror, 1927

As soon as it became clear that the Northern Expedition would be ultimately successful against the warlords, Chiang renewed his attack on the Communists. This reached its climax in the 'White Terror' in Shanghai in April 1927. Shanghai had witnessed the growth of a powerful trade union movement under the direction of Zhou Enlai, and the formation of a workers' army that was so effective that it had been able to undermine the local warlord's attempt to prevent the advance of Chiang's Nationalist forces. Only days after entering the city, Chiang turned savagely on the very people who had earlier given him a hero's welcome. Backed by Shanghai's industrialists and merchants who were eager to crush the trade unions, and by those living in the international settlements, who were fearful of the growing tide of anti-foreigner demonstrations, Chiang's troops went on the rampage. Using the information passed to them by the city's triads and underworld gangsters, they rooted out and shot 5,000 known Communists and their sympathisers. Similar anti-Communist coups were carried out by Chiang's GMD armies in a number of other cities, including Guangzhou.

Despite attempts to resist, including the unsuccessful Autumn Harvest Rising led by Mao Zedong in September, the CCP was in a

Execution of Communists during the White Terror in Shanghai, 1927

desperate plight by the end of 1927. Its members survived only by fleeing to the sanctuary of the mountains of Jiangxi (Kiangsi), this in rejection of the Comintern's orders to stay and maintain the Front. The GMD forces pursued the Communists into Jiangxi. For the next seven years the remnants of the CCP were to be engaged in a struggle to survive against continual Nationalist harassment.

4 The Jiangxi Soviet, 1928-34

Mao Zedong arrived in Jiangxi with certain advantages over his CCP rivals. His denunciation of the now discredited United Front had added greatly to his political reputation, while that of leaders such as Chen Duxui (Chen Tu-hsiu), who had advocated maintaining the Front, had correspondingly diminished. According to Mao's own writings, the White Terror had confirmed a judgement to which his experience as party organiser among the workers and peasants in Hunan province had already led him; namely, that co-operation with the GMD would destroy the Chinese Communist movement. He resolved that the CCP must revert to being a separate independent force. This was not merely because of Chiang's murderous intentions, but because the United Front's revolutionary policy was based on a false reading of the situation in China. The GMD under direction from the Comintern had adopted a strategy of urban revolution, which the CCP had then sanctioned by its willingness to form the Front. Yet for Mao the real China was not urban but rural. It was a simple matter of population distribution. The Front's policy of fomenting insurrection in the cities and towns ignored an essential reality - the great mass of the Chinese people were peasants living in the countryside.

The official CCP line has always been to accept Mao's statements regarding his opposition to the United Front at face value. His prescience has been customarily lauded on two counts: first, that he saw through the machinations of the GMD which was simply concerned to establish its own dominance; second, that he was committed to the furtherance of revolution in the countryside not the towns, calculating that in the prevailing conditions effective resistance in the urban areas was impossible. However, more recent analyses suggest that Mao's description may have been a matter of *post facto* self-justification. Mao did not become fully committed to rural revolution until the late 1920s, after his experience of the CCP's failure in the towns. Moreover, he appears to have been fully supportive of the Front until its threat to the CCP became clearly evident with the launching of Chiang Kaishek's White Terror in 1927.

Regardless of the arguments about the precise timing of Mao's conversion to the the notion of peasant revolution, what is true is that the statistics undeniably bear out the accuracy of his judgement. The figures for 1933 show the following:

Total Population of China - 500 million

distribution: urban centres larger than 50,000   - 30 million (6%)
                 areas between 10,000 and 50,000   - 30 million (6%)
                 rural areas   - 440 million (88%)

Total Work Force - 259 million

distribution: 205 million   - agricultural workers
                  51 million   - non-agricultural workers
                   3 million   - industrial workers

Mao, unimpressed by Soviet Marxist orthodoxy and in defiance of Comintern instructions, made the peasants the dynamic of the Chinese revolution. In his own words: 'If we allot ten points to the revolution, then the urban dwellers rate only three points, while the remaining seven points must go to the peasants'. It was Mao's belief in the truly revolutionary potential of the peasantry that inspired his organisation of the CCP's Jiangxi base between 1928 and 1934. In this period he taught his small but growing band of Reds that there was no necessity to wait for the growth of an industrial proletariat in China. Genuine revolution would be achieved by the peasants.

1 Within a short time, hundreds of millions of peasants will rise in Central, South, and North China with the fury of a hurricane; no power, however strong, can restrain them. They will break all the shackles that bind them and rush towards the road of liberation.
5 All imperialists, warlords, corrupt officials, and bad gentry will meet their doom at the hands of the peasants. All revolutionary parties and comrades will be judged by them.

He told his CCP followers that it was their task to unleash the huge potential of the peasantry: 'The peasants are the sea; we are the fish. The sea is our habitat'. Mao had already begun the process of shaping Marxism to fit the Chinese situation. This put him at variance with the orthodox urban Communists, such as Li Lisan and Chen Duxui, who continued to follow the Moscow line in asserting that revolution was a dialectical progression whose stages could not be skipped at will. Frequent attempts were made by the hardliners to make Mao conform. He was accused of 'reckless adventurism'. Yet, Mao as leader of the Jiangxi soviet was recruiting peasants into the ranks of the party at a rate unmatched in any other CCP-held areas. He was winning the argument in a very practical way. The truth was that it was not in the cities but in the countryside that the CCP was making its gains. The urban

Communists began to be appear increasingly out of touch with the real situation in China. Their orthodox theories counted for little in the face of Mao's heterodox but manifestly successful approach.

In insisting on the correctness of his interpretations and in fighting for his position within the party, Mao showed a ferocity of purpose which remained a key feature throughout his career. A striking example of this was the 'Futien incident' in 1930 when he conducted a two-month campaign against a rival unit within the Jiangxi Red Army whom he suspected of being either GMD agents or supporters of Li Lisan. In the course of crushing what he regarded as a military and political revolt, Mao Zedong ordered the execution of nearly 3,000 officers and men. Maoist sympathisers have argued that rather than being an example of Mao's vindictiveness, Futien illustrates his grip on realities and his willingness to take hard decisions, qualities without which he could not have survived in the desperate circumstances within which he operated. Less sympathetic commentators regard Futien as an expression of Mao's ruthless determination to eliminate rivals who blocked his path to personal power. They point to a particularly sinister aspect of Mao's tactics - his use of secret police to root out and expose the ringleaders of the revolt.

The CCP's internal rivalries took place against the background of the GMD's constant effort to crush the Jiangxi base. Chiang, who was similarly troubled by factional difficulties within his own party, was nonetheless resolute in his pursuit of the Communists. Beginning in the late 1920s, he adopted, on the recommendation of his German military advisers, a series of encirclement campaigns aimed at denying resources to the Reds until they finally broke. The basic tactic was to blockade the Communists into an ever-shrinking area by means of pillboxes and manned road blocks across the approaches to the CCP strongholds. This massive siege began to work. By 1934 a succession of serious defeats for the Reds convinced Mao that to continue to defend the Jiangxi base would prove suicidal. He was no more prepared to take heed of those in the party who argued that they should stay and die as revolutionary heroes than he had been at the time of the White Terror seven years earlier. The decision was taken to transfer to a safer region, but since the only viable base lay at Yanan in remote Shaanxi province, thousands of miles to the north, the Reds had to undertake what proved to be one of the great odysseys of history, the Long March. In a pretence that the decision to flee Jiangxi was made freely rather than being forced upon them by the GMD's encirclement, the CCP announced that 'the Chinese Red Army of workers and peasants has chosen to march North to resist the Japanese'. The main body of marchers set off in October 1934.

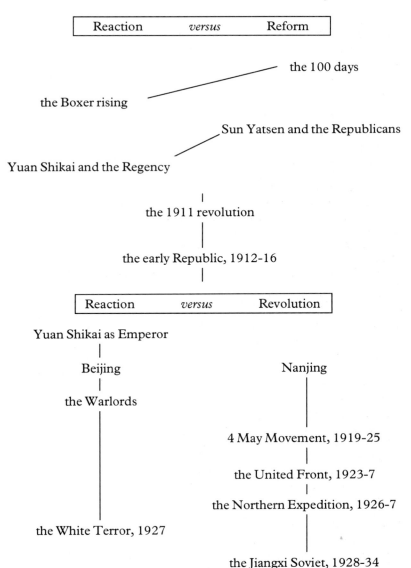

Reaction	*versus*	Reform

the 100 days

the Boxer rising

Sun Yatsen and the Republicans

Yuan Shikai and the Regency

the 1911 revolution

the early Republic, 1912-16

Reaction	*versus*	Revolution

Yuan Shikai as Emperor

Beijing   Nanjing

the Warlords

4 May Movement, 1919-25

the United Front, 1923-7

the Northern Expedition, 1926-7

the White Terror, 1927

the Jiangxi Soviet, 1928-34

Summary - Civil Strife in China, 1900-34

CHAPTER 3

Civil Strife in China, 1934-49

1 The Long March, 1934-5

The Long March has become the stuff of legend. Even after allowing for exaggeration it remains an extraordinary feat. The journey, which covered the year from October 1934 to October 1935, involved crossing 11 provinces, 18 mountain ranges, 24 rivers, and numerous desert areas and quick sands. The marchers fought 15 pitched battles and almost daily skirmishes against the GMD forces trying to destroy them. In the course of the march, over 60 towns and cities were occupied. The distance covered was 6,000 miles - the equivalent of marching from London to Lagos, or New York to Los Angeles and back, at an average of 17 miles per day. Of the 100,000 who set out scarcely 20,000 survived to reach Yanan. The sheer physical scale of the Long March helped to give it a political significance, which Mao defined in these terms:

1 It is a manifesto, an agitation corps, a seeding machine ... It
  proclaims to the world that the Red Army is an army of heroes ... It
  announces the bankruptcy of the encirclement attempted by the
  imperialists and Chiang Kaishek ... It declares to approximately
5 200 million people of 11 provinces that only the road of the Red
  Army leads to their liberation ... It has sown many seeds in 11
  provinces, which will sprout, grow leaves, blossom into flowers,
  bear fruit and yield a crop in future ... the Long March ended with
  our victory and the enemy's defeat.

The concept of martyrdom for the cause became enshrined in Communist lore. Comradeship, dedication and self-sacrifice were now the watchwords of the party. The March created a brotherhood among the survivors; all the leaders of the Chinese People's Republic from 1949 until the mid-1990s were veterans of the Long March: Mao Zedong, Zhu De, Zhou Enlai, Lin Biao, Liu Shaoqi, Jiang Qing and Deng Xiaoping. The marchers, with their willingness to accept privation and suffering without complaint, were an extraordinary invocation of the Confucian spirit of fatalism. The poems Mao wrote during the March were very much in the Chinese literary tradition of embracing nature as a measure of human achievement:

1 I desire to compare our height with the skies;
  In clear weather, the earth is so charming,
  Like a red-faced girl clothed in white.
  Such is the charm of these rivers and mountains,
5 Calling innumerable heroes to vie with each other in pursuing her.
  The emperors Shih Huang and Wu Ti were barely cultured,

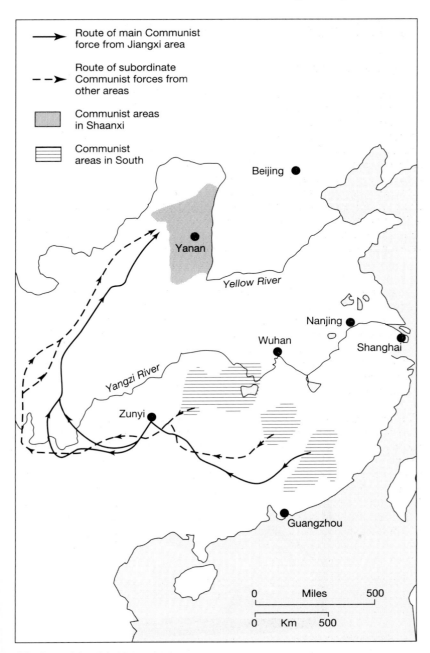

Route of main Communist
force from Jiangxi area

Route of subordinate
Communist forces from
other areas

Communist areas
in Shaanxi

Communist
areas in South

Beijing

Yanan

Yellow River

Nanjing

Wuhan

Shanghai

Yangzi River

Zunyi

Guangzhou

0   Miles   500

0   Km   500

The Long March 1934-5

The emperors Tai Tsung and Tai Tsu were lacking in feeling,
Genghis Khan knew only how to bend his bow at the eagles.
These all belong to the past - only today are there men of feeling!

Mao Zedong had not been the only leader of the March, but he was the one who emerged from it with the greatest prestige among his fellow Communists. By the time they reached Yanan he had achieved a remarkable supremacy in the military and political counsels of the CCP. During the March what proved to be a crucial party gathering had been held at Zunyi (Tsunyi) in Guizhou (Kweichow) province early in 1935. At the meeting Mao successfully exposed the urban Reds as being out of touch with the CCP's real needs. His principal charge was that they had reduced the party to its present crisis by abandoning the successful guerilla tactics in the countryside and opting instead for pitched battles in the urban areas. In a key vote on the issue the majority of the members supported Mao, a decision that marked the end of the predominating influence of the pro-Moscow urban element in the CCP.

There had also been a serious dispute over the route the Red armies should follow. Zhang Guotao (Chang Kuo-tao), a rival to Mao, urged that the marchers divert westwards through Xinjiang (Sinkiang) in order to take them closer to Russian protection. Mao, backed by Zhu De (Chuh Teh), insisted that the agreed northern route should be

Drawing of the Long March by one of the marchers, 1935

maintained. Zhang broke away but after some months had to admit that the western route he had attempted was impossible. He abandoned it and rejoined Mao's contingent on its northern march. This vindication of Mao's strategic judgement, increased his standing within the CCP and meant that he arrived at Yanan as the leading figure in the party.

The romantic image of the Long March tends to obscure the fact that at the time it was widely seen as a defeat for the Communists. After all, they had been driven out of their southern base and in the course of their flight had lost four-fifths of their number. As in 1927 at the time of the White Terror, so in 1935 the Nationalists seemed on the point of establishing an unshakeable control of China: Chiang Kaishek and the GMD had been recognised by the Western powers and the USSR as the legitimate government of China, the warlord menace had been subdued and the Communists appeared to be a broken force, confined to a distant province. Although the Nationalists did not yet have total power, they possessed the greatest degree of authority of any group since the fall of the Manchus. The question was would they be able to use that authority to consolidate their position. The answer to that depended on two key factors, the presence of the Japanese in China and the attitude of Chiang Kaishek.

2 The Xian Incident, 1936

Japan's aggressive designs on China had been openly declared in 1931 with the invasion of Manchuria. That proved to be the first step in a programme of Japanese expansion that was to lead to open war between the two countries from 1937 to 1945. During those eight years large areas of China were occupied by the Japanese. Ironically, this proved the saving of Mao Zedong and the Communists, for it was they who took on the role of the real defenders of the nation against the aggressor, a role which the GMD under Chiang Kaishek seemed unwilling to fulfil. Although Chiang formally committed his government to the anti-Japanese struggle, he continued throughout the war to make his priority the elimination of the Communists. One of the major criticisms to be made of Chiang was that his obsession with crushing the Reds diverted the Nationalists from attending to China's more urgent problems. Resources were dissipated on anti-Communist campaigns which should have been devoted to China's economic recovery or to its anti-Japanese war effort. It is certainly the case that throughout the period of Nationalist control Chiang's preoccupation with the Communist threat condemned China to a continuous civil war at the very time it was engaged in a fight for survival against Japan. The CCP denounced Chiang's failure to conform to the promise he had originally made when entering the United Front; they stressed that while they were prepared to confront the Japanese, the GMD invariably adopted the line of least resistance.

Chiang's strategy against Japan derived from his belief that China was too large a country for the Japanese to occupy without exhausting themselves; a protracted war must end in Japan's defeat. He defined his approach as 'selling space to buy time'. However, the policy of avoiding engagement with the invader proved uninspiring and brought obvious political dangers. His supporters frequently found it difficult to maintain their loyalty. Throughout his time as leader of the GMD, Chiang was subject to opposition from within its ranks. In 1933 it took him over a year to suppress a rising among his troops at Fujian (Fukien), who were reacting against his failure to confront the Japanese. Open criticism of the GMD's irresolute war policy was sustained by a series of demonstrations in Beijing, the most serious occurring in 1935. The climax to Chiang Kaishek's discomfiture came in a remarkable episode in 1936. During a visit to Xian, which, ironically, Chiang had undertaken in order to berate his GMD forces for their slowness in crushing the Reds, he found the tables turned; he was seized by troops acting under the orders of General Zhang Xue-liang (Chang Hsueh-liang). Zhang had been persuaded by the CCP to commit himself to the anti-Japanese struggle and to use his contacts with the Nationalists to embarrass Chiang. After his arrest Chiang was handed over to Zhou Enlai, Mao's closest colleague, who offered to spare his prisoner's life if he would promise to end his persecution of the CCP and lead a genuine resistance against the Japanese. Finding himself in an impossible position, Chiang Kaishek gave in; in December 1936, he sanctioned the formation of the second GMD-CCP United Front, pledged to wage unceasing war against the Japanese aggressors.

Given the bitter relations between Chiang and the Communists, it is at first sight surprising that the CCP did not simply assassinate him; that after all would have been normal Chinese politics. That they refrained from doing so suggests an interesting degree of subtlety on their part. They took a calculated risk that paid off. By allowing Chiang not merely to survive, but to remain as the recognised leader of China, the CCP had won a major propaganda victory. They had shown remarkable restraint in forgoing party advantage for the sake of the nation. They had obtained Chiang's formal commitment to cease his suppression of the CCP, as well as his promise to lead a new united front against the Japanese invader. The Communists could now claim that it was they who were the genuine nationalists whose prime motivation was their love of China. They had undermined the validity of the GMD's claim to represent the nation.

3 The Communists at Yanan, 1936-45

Detached from Comintern interference and close to the Japanese lines, the CCP base at Yanan provided the Reds with a remarkable opportunity both to develop an independent political programme and to assume the role of defenders of the Chinese people. Mao was able to give practical form to his belief that China's revolution must come from the peasants. This was heresy in the eyes of the Comintern; to them the CCP was too small and historically out of phase. Since China lacked an established proletariat, it was incapable of creating a genuinely proletarian revolution. The best that the CCP could achieve would be to help bring about the bourgeois stage of revolution by merging with the Nationalists. Peasant revolution was not an end in itself; it was merely the precursor of the final proletarian revolution. Mao rejected this analysis and replaced it with his own conviction that for China the people's peasant rising would be sufficient to fulfil the dialectical imperative. He tended to despise the purely intellectual approach to revolution which emphasised theoretical concepts without taking sufficient account of the actual conditions in China. For him, the term proletarian described not so much a social class as an attitude. Those who were genuinely committed to revolution were *ipso facto* members of the proletariat.

That was very much the spirit that prevailed at Yanan from 1936 onwards. Aided by the base's distance from Soviet influence, Mao was able to dominate the urban-orientated members of the CCP and bring the party to accept his line of thinking. He was acting very much in the Chinese tradition of taking from a foreign ideology those elements considered to be of practical value for China. Under him Marxism became Sinified. For some years he had to contend with opposition from within the party concerning his reordering of revolutionary Marxism, but by outmanoeuvring and, where necessary, removing opponents he was able to establish an unmatched authority and so impose his ideas. Mao had few scruples about how he achieved this. It is known that he tightened his political grip by the use of informers and secret police. There is no reason to believe that in the story of Mao's rise to power in the CCP the Futien incident was an isolated occurrence.

During the Jiangxi and Yanan years Mao's tactics for imposing CCP control in the countryside were essentially simple. Once the Reds had infiltrated or seized a village the landowners were driven out or shot. This done, the land was immediately reallocated to the peasants, thereby making them supporters of the CCP soviet that was then established. The character of the land expropriation and distribution policy may be judged from the following extracts from the CCP's Land Law of 1932:

1   *A. Whose Land Should be Confiscated?*
    Land, houses, and all forms of property that belonged to members
    of the gentry and landlords.
    Land and farm implements owned by those rich peasants who have
5   been verified as members of counterrevolutionary organisations.
    B. Who Should Receive Land?
    The amount of land to be distributed is the same for all tenant

farmers and poor peasants. Whether the land of the middle
peasants should be distributed so as to assure that they have the
10 same amount as that of tenant farmers and poor peasants depends
upon the decision to be made by the middle peasants themselves. If
the majority of them so desires, the land of the middle peasants will
be redistributed.

C. *How is Land to be Redistributed?*
15 Insofar as tenant farmers, poor and middle peasants, unemployed
farm labourers, and unemployed independent artisans are
concerned, population and land productivity shall be taken into
consideration.

No government official in any of the revolutionary organisations is
20 entitled to land distribution if he is not a tenant farmer, poor or
middle peasant, unemployed farm labourer, coolie, or independent artisan.

D. *How Is Land to be Distributed Among Members of the Red Army?*
The relatives of a Red soldier will receive land in the same manner
25 as poor and middle peasants. The land they receive shall not be
located too far from where they live.

What the CCP's occupation of what it called the 'liberated areas'

Trial of a landlord by the Red Army, 1949

actually entailed was described by Edgar Snow, an American
Communist, who travelled with the Red Army and became a confidant
of Mao Zedong. Writing in 1938, Snow observed:

1 While theoretically the soviets were a 'workers and peasants'
government, in actual practice the whole constituency was
overwhelmingly peasant in character. Various committees were
established under each of the district soviets. An all-powerful
5 committee, usually elected in a mass meeting shortly after the
occupation of a district by the Red Army, and preceded by an
intensified propaganda campaign, was the revolutionary committee. It called for elections or re-elections, and closely co-operated
with the Communist Party. Under the district soviet, and
10 appointed by it, were committees for education, co-operatives,
military training, political training, land, public health, partisan
training, revolutionary defence, enlargement of the Red Army,
agrarian mutual aid, Red Army land tilling, and others. Such
committees were found in every branch organ of the soviets, right
15 up to the Central government, where policies were co-ordinated
and state decisions made.
   The work of all these organizations and their various
committees was co-ordinated by the Central Soviet Government,
the Communist Party, and the Red Army. It can be said in general
20 that they were all skilfully interwoven, and each directly under the
guidance of some Communist, though decisions on organization,
membership, and work seemed to be carried out in a democratic
way by the peasants themselves. The aim of soviet organization
obviously was to make every man, woman, or child a member of
25 something, with definite work assigned to him to perform.

At Yanan Mao urged that the first task for the CCP was to consolidate
itself as a military force. This was not only in order to be able to fight
Japan and the Nationalists, but also because, as the Long March had so
graphically shown, the Red Army was the party's major political
weapon. It was the means by which the word was to be spread. Until the
Yanan period, the Chinese soldier had not stood high in popular
estimation; recruited from the dregs of society, he had traditionally been
a terror to the civilian population. The marauding imperial and warlord
armies had wrought fearful havoc among the peasantry. But the Red
Army was different. Its prescribed duty was to aid and comfort the
people. Mao laid down a code of conduct for his troops:

1 1. Replace all doors when you leave a house.
  2. Roll up and return the straw matting on which you sleep.
  3. Be courteous and help out when you can.
  4. Return all borrowed articles.

5 5. Replace all damaged articles.
   6. Be honest in all transactions with the peasants.
   7. Pay for all articles purchased.
   8. Be sanitary, and especially establish latrines at a distance from
      people's houses.
10 9. Don't take liberties with women.
   10. Don't kill prisoners of war.

Many of these instructions may have a naive, boy-scout, tone to them
yet they provided a guide which when followed endeared the Red Army
to a rural population whose previous experience of marching armies had
been unremittingly bitter. The political role played by the Red Army
during the Yanan years was part of what Mao described as 'the new
democracy'. In a series of reflections, which were published in 1940
under the title *On New Democracy*, Mao defined the revolution which
the Chinese Communists were leading not as a class movement but as a
national one. The aim of the Communists was 'long-term co-operation
with all those classes, strata, political groups and individuals who were
willing to fight Japan to the end'. He appealed to all Chinese of goodwill
to unite against the enemies of the nation. To encourage unity, Mao
chose to play down the political threat that the Communists represented
to the provincial landowners. The CCP's former land-confiscation
programme was modified so that only those landlords who actively
collaborated with the Japanese had their property seized. At the same
time Mao was careful not to depart from the party's policy of forcing
down excessive rents and prohibiting the usury that had so often
blighted the lives of the peasants. These programmes were often effected
through CCP co-operation with the local peasant associations, a
technique which encouraged non-party members to feel that they were
directly responsible for improving their own lot. The same applied to the
literacy and education schemes that the CCP introduced. Undoubtedly
this sensitivity to the wants of the peasants was the most popular of the
CCP's policies and played its part in the growth of the party from 40,000
in 1937 to 1 million by 1945. It was from this expanding membership
that the volunteers for the Red Army came.

Historical balance requires that such admiring descriptions as Edgar
Snow's of the CCP's organisation of the peasants be matched by
reference to Nationalist denunciations of Mao's policies. The removal of
the landlord class in the areas where the Red Army held sway could be a
brutal process. C.W. Young, A western spokesman for the GMD, wrote
in 1935 of the Communists' 'indescribable reign of Terror':

> The populace was forced to undergo unnecessary hardships and
> suffering and to live a life of bondage, a veritable nightmare,
> instead of receiving equality and benefits and good treatment such
> as they had been led to believe they would receive.

While this might be viewed as Nationalist propaganda rather than objective reporting, it needs to be borne in mind that, notwithstanding its feeling for the ordinary Chinese and its genuine popularity, Mao's regime was politically authoritarian. There was a rigour and sense of purpose about the atmosphere at Yanan that bordered on the oppressive. Discipline and obedience to instructions were required of all those living under it. In one sense this was understandable, given that the regime was engaged in a constant fight for survival against both the Japanese and the GMD. But it went deeper than that. Mao had begun to manifest a belief that was to become his outstanding political characteristic - the notion of revolutionary correctness. He held that unless the party maintained a constant struggle against error the revolution would be betrayed from within. For Mao, an obvious danger was that those responsible for running the party would become a bureaucratic, self-justifying elite. To fight this tendency, in 1942 he launched a 'rectification of conduct' campaign. Party members were to engage in public self-criticism. To assist them in their search for revolutionary truth they were obliged to study prescribed texts, among which Mao's own writings figured prominently.

Historians have argued over the motive behind Mao's campaign. Some see it as a logical part of his progression as a revolutionary thinker. Others view the campaign as a calculated move to rid himself of opposition and consolidate his position as leader. What is certainly true is that by 1942 Mao had already begun to move towards cult status in Yanan, and the rectification campaign with its emphasis on the wisdom of his ideas obviously added to this. In 1943 Mao was elected Chairman of the Central Committee of the CCP; by 1945 when the Japanese war came to an end, Mao was being regularly referred to as 'the great helmsman'.

4 Nationalist China, 1937-45

The GMD's power in China was always more apparent than real. At no time did the Nationalist government control more than one-third of China or two-thirds of its population. These, of course, were quite substantial proportions in themselves, but given the strength of Chinese regionalism and the distribution of the population the authority exercised by the GMD was far from complete. A clear example of this was the Nanjing government's failure, in the face of resistance from the local ruling factions, to carry through its declared policies of land reform and equitable rents. Moreover, despite the impressive victories of the Northern Expedition, the defeat of warlordism was only partial. A number of the warlords had agreed to accept the GMD's authority only on condition that they were allowed to keep their private armies. Others were won over by being offered executive positions in the party or government.

It is arguable, therefore, that the Nationalists did not so much conquer the warlords as come to terms with them. This was the constant assertion made by the CCP in its propaganda against the Nationalists. A further obvious limitation of GMD authority was the Japanese control of large parts of China between 1931 and 1945. That the Nationalists had to remove their capital city inland from Nanjing (Nanking) to Chongqing (Chungking) was an outstanding illustration of this. The fourteen-year occupation by Japanese armies was a violent and humiliating reminder of how far China was from being an independent nation.

The underlying political weakness of the GMD was that the social composition of its membership meant that it could never become a mass party. The GMD claimed that its revolutionary purpose was to serve the Chinese population as a whole, but in practice it became the representative of particular minority interests. Chiang Kaishek's party was largely drawn from the entrepreneurial capitalist class of China, congregated in the ports and cities. These urban merchants and businessmen had little sympathy for the rural peasants. The character of the party was manifest in the manner in which it acquired its finance. Over 90 per cent of the revenue raised by the Nationalist government came from the area around Shanghai, China's largest international port and money market. Yet the revenue was not well used. Throughout its whole period in office, the government's most pressing need was to fund its war effort. Almost all that it raised went on military expenditure, which left a minimal amount for the vital areas of industrial investment and agrarian reform.

In political terms the GMD's lack of genuine popularity might have mattered less had they been able to satisfy the demands of the particular interests they were thought to represent. However, rather than forge a partnership with China's business interests, the Nationalist government tried to make those interests dependent on it for their freedom to trade while at the same time denying them access to political influence. The GMD's governmental elite were not prepared to share their power even with their natural supporters. The record shows that the government's ill-conceived policies forfeited the goodwill of the financial and business classes, the very groups on which a genuine modernisation of China depended. The government tried to acquire the money it needed by nationalising China's private banks and imposing heavy taxation on individual and company profits. But since it invariably spent more than it raised, it also had to resort to borrowing from foreign financiers, usually American. The GMD government was leading China towards bankruptcy.

After 1935 the GMD had a whole decade of opportunity to shape China in accordance with their revolutionary programme. Judged by this, their record was an uninspiring one. They operated an inefficient bureaucracy which easily fell prey to corruption. Intent on gaining

American dollars, the GMD government in China compromised most of its professed revolutionary values. Having started as a party dedicated to the rejection of foreign dominance over China, the GMD, from the 1930s on, modelled itself in practice on the capitalist methods of the Western merchants and financiers whom it had previously affected to despise. It was no accident that many of its leaders, including Chiang himself, either married or ingratiated themselves into the social circles associated with Western capitalism. Chiang's second marriage to Soong Mei-ling, sister-in-law of Sun Yatsen and daughter to one of China's richest and most influential families, was a calculated step to make himself more acceptable to the Americans. Similarly, his avowal of Christian Methodism may be interpreted as an attempt to impress Western opinion.

Yet Chiang's adoption of Western values did not extend into the political field. Despite their constant avowals of dedication to the 3 Principles of the People, the Nationalists made few real concessions to democracy and paid scant attention to providing for the welfare of the people. The sacrifice and commitment to the nation which Chiang called for in his *China's Destiny*, published in 1943 as a textbook of the revolutionary ideals of the party, were rarely found in the conduct of public life under him. Although the Communists exaggerated the extent of corruption in the Nationalist ranks, there was no denying that during the Nationalist years public office was bought and sold and nepotism was the main means of advancement.

This corruption provided the CCP with a powerful political weapon in its conflict with Chiang Kaishek. The Communists were not above committing unscrupulous acts themselves, but the general perception was that not only were they steadfast in their resistance to Japanese aggression but that they also behaved with genuine integrity in their political dealings. This may now be judged a misconception, but what mattered at the time was how the ordinary Chinese saw things. For many of them the Communist refusal to engage in the traditional brutalising of the population was proof that the CCP was sincere in its claims to be truly concerned with the fate of the Chinese people. The difference in the ways the leaders of the GMD and the CCP treated their troops could not have been more marked. The President of the Chinese Red Cross was appalled by the barbarity suffered by the Nationalist conscripts. In a formal report he recorded:

1 In one reception centre, I met a group of draftees from Kwantung. 'How many draftees are there in your group?' 'There were 700 of us at the beginning of the journey. Now only seventeen have remained.' 'Are you telling me that all but seventeen have
5 successfully escaped on the road?' 'No, sir', they replied. 'Where could they run away to on the road? The areas we passed through were nothing but wilderness where one could not find food or

water. We had no food with us when we started the journey, and
we had to survive on whatever we could find on the road. When we
10 could not find anything, we, of course, starved. In some areas
water was so contaminated that we suffered from diarrhoea the
moment we drank it. Since no medicine was available, people died
in droves.'

In many of the reception centres that I had visited, the draftees
15 were tied to one another to forestall any possible escape. They had
no freedom of movement whatsoever. They would be immediately
whipped if, in the judgment of their officers, they had misbehaved.
The food they ate was not only crude to the greatest extreme but
also inadequate in quantity. Its only function was to prevent them
20 from starving to death. Under cruel treatment like this, many of
them died before they could even be sent to the front.

In Yunnan province, I saw a group of army recruiters gambling
with large stakes. Being occupied with what they were doing at the
moment, they paid little attention to the draftees who, being sick
25 and lying beside them, were on the verge of death. One draftee
pleaded hopefully: "Give me some water, please; I am so thirsty
that I am about to die." Instead of showing any sympathy, these
army recruiters scolded him in angry voice: "Get out of here! Why
do you always want to make trouble?"
30   Cruelties like this appeared time and again during my inspection
tour. The lack of sympathy on the part of army recruiters was
almost universal. According to my estimate, the total number of
draftees who died from a variety of causes during the eight years of
war (1937-45) was no less than 14 million.

5 The Civil War, 1945-9

By a strange twist of history, what should have been Chiang's
moment of triumph proved to be the beginning of his downfall. The
surrender of Japan in August 1945, directly following the atomic
bombing of Hiroshima and Nagasaki, was in one obvious sense a
great Chinese victory. Japan had been defeated. But it had not come
the way that Chiang had expected. The war had ended too soon. His
belief throughout had been that the fanatical Japanese resistance
would eventually lead to two critical developments: first, the setting
up of US air bases in China from which the Americans would attack
Japan; second, the landing in China of huge American armies, which
would roll up the Japanese in a large land operation. Chiang
calculated that in the course of this the Americans would overwhelm
not only the Japanese but the Chinese Communists as well. This
would leave him both the victor over Japan and the master of China.

But events betrayed him. The Americans chose to establish their
airbases not in China but on the Pacific islands that they wrested from

Japan. Then, when the war abruptly ended in August 1945, the location of the Japanese and their Communist resisters meant that it was invariably the Reds to whom the Japanese formally submitted. The events of 1945 had thus destroyed Chiang Kaishek's dream. He did not have the expected American troops at his disposal in China, which prevented him from crushing the Communists as he had planned. A further limitation on Chiang's claim to mastery of China was that Russian armies had now occupied Manchuria, the USSR having declared war on Japan the day after the Nagasaki bombing. It is true that the Americans then provided a massive airlift to enable the GMD to transport its forces to the northern cities so as to be in a position to take the Japanese surrender. But by then the war was over and the CCP resisted the GMD's claim to the liberated areas, which during the years of anti-Japanese struggle had become Communist administered zones.

CCP-GMD hostility mounted and the USA felt constrained to attempt to bring the sides together. In 1945, for the first time in twenty years, Chiang and Mao Zedong met personally. In October 1945 it was announced that the two leaders had reached an agreement. But it could not last; after two decades of animosity neither was willing to accept the other's authority. By 1946 the civil war which had continued intermittently during the years of Japanese occupation had broken out into a full-scale conflict.

The renewed civil war soon revealed how shrunken the GMD's popular support had become. It was a crippling weakness for which not even the resources that Chiang Kaishek continued to receive from the USA could compensate. The initial aim of the Nationalists was to move north to enlarge their area of control which had hitherto been restricted to southern China. However, this required that the Communists be driven from the liberated areas they held. It was the GMD's attempt to achieve this that marked the renewal of open hostilities. At the beginning, Chiang's 5 million troops outnumbered those of the CCP by over four to one. In addition, the GMD's military resources and equipment, much of which was supplied by the USA, were far superior. But these advantages were more than balanced by the higher morale and superior strategy of the Communists. Able to live off the land and confident of the support of the rural peoples among whom they moved, the CCP armies simply by-passed the main GMD strongholds, avoiding set battles unless troop dispositions were in their favour. Mao's strategy was expressed in a mantra that all his troops knew by heart. 'When the enemy advances, we retreat. When the enemy escapes, we harass. When they retreat, we pursue. When they tire, we attack'.

After some seemingly impressive successes in the first year of the war, including the taking of Yanan, the Nationalists were unable to achieve a single major victory between 1947 and 1949. Faced by growing desertions, even among the higher ranks of the officers, and a deepening war weariness in the GMD-held areas, Chiang increasingly resorted to coercion. Property was seized, money expropriated, and enlistment enforced. Protesters were arrested in large numbers and summary executions became commonplace. In August 1948, Shanghai witnessed particularly bloody scenes, including street-corner beheadings and shootings by government troops. Such atrocities alienated the Nationalists' diminishing band of supporters and dismayed their foreign apologists, most significantly the Americans. Splits occurred in the GMD ranks; rival factions opposed to Chiang, such as the Guomindang Revolutionary Alliance and the Democratic League came into being. Against this background it became progressively more difficult for Chiang's Nationalists to sustain their war effort.

Three major battles may be judged to have determined the military outcome of the CCP-GMD conflict. The defeat of the Nationalists at Mukden (Shenyang) in November 1948 meant in effect the loss of China north of Beijing. This was followed a month later by the Communist victory at Hsuchow, a key railway junction, whose fall left the CCP in control of the central provinces. Then in January 1949 the surrender of Beijing to the Communists finally pushed the Nationalists beyond the point of recovery. The last nine months of the war were a mopping-up exercise for the CCP. Nanjing, Shanghai, and Guangzhou had all fallen by the time the Chinese People's Republic was formally

Shooting of a Communist agent by GMD police, 1949

declared by Mao Zedong at the entrance to the Forbidden City in Beijing in October 1949. By then Chiang Kaishek had already fled with the remnants of his forces to the island of Taiwan. There he established a Nationalist stronghold which continued to claim to be the legitimate government of the whole of China.

6 Reasons for the Communist Victory in 1949

Although it was not appreciated by the outside world and probably not even by Chiang and the Nationalists, by the time the Japanese war ended in 1945 the CCP had, in effect, won the civil war. It was true that there would be another four years' bitter fighting, but what Mao called the 'the struggle for the hearts of the people' was already effectively over.

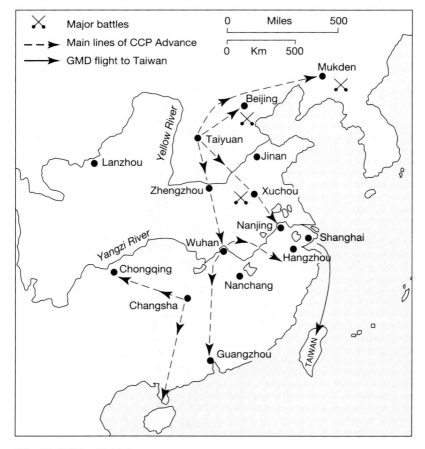

The Civil War 1946-9

Against Chiang's corruption, factionalism, detachment from China's fundamental needs, and dependence on foreign aid, Mao could offer involvement in the genuine aspirations of the nation, sympathy with the masses of the Chinese peasantry, and an unequivocally nationalist resistance to the enemy. General Joseph Stilwell, the American wartime liaison officer, was in a position to observe the situation in China at first hand. A fierce critic of Chiang and the Nationalists, 'Vinegar Joe' had reported as early as 1943:

> 1 I judge Guomindang and Communist Party by what I saw: GMD -
>   Corruption, neglect, chaos, economy, taxes, words and deeds.
>   Hoarding, black market, trading with the enemy. Communist
>   program ... reduce taxes, rents, interest. Raise production and
> 5 standard of living. Participate in government. Practice [sic] what
>   they preach.

By a striking irony the CCP had come far closer to fulfilling the 3 Principles of the People than had the Nationalists. They had united a large part of the nation in resistance to the Japanese. In their 'liberated areas' they had created political structures which, though rudimentary by Western standards provided for the first time effective administration in the countryside. The local population had been encouraged through their peasant associations and co-operatives to participate in the organisation of their own affairs.

After 1945 the GMD's great political weakness was that they had had ten years of government in which to prove the validity of their claims. That decade had been distinguished by administrative inefficiency and self-seeking. The achievements of the time were small and unremarkable in the eyes of contemporaries. The Communists were able to portray themselves as essentially different; their willingness to co-operate with the GMD, despite the latter's murderous inclination to destroy its opponents, suggested a high degree of selflessness. Communist front-line resistance to the Japanese armies was spoken of as an inspiring refusal to accept the centuries of humiliation that the foreigner had perpetrated against the Chinese. The land policy followed by the CCP could be said to be unique in its readiness to heed the wishes and needs of the local communities. These were potent propaganda weapons that the Communists were able to turn against Chiang and his Nationalists.

In contrast to the ineptitude of the Nationalist government, Mao Zedong, by virtue of his organising ability and awesome power to inspire others, had won the loyalty of a large part of the population in the face of what often appeared to be impossible odds. Recent research does suggest that he employed the most unscrupulous methods to maintain himself as leader of the CCP during its troubled days on the run. In many respects his rectification campaign at Yanan recalled the brainwashing and terror tactics associated with Stalin's purges in the USSR. Mao was also quite prepared to use brutal methods in the countryside. Indeed, some historians explain the popularity of the CCP among the peasants by reference to the licence the party gave them to seize the property of their hated landlords. Others suggest that it is all part of the essentially expedient policies that Mao Zedong pursued. In areas where it paid to be moderate in order to win the support of the local gentry, the CCP was quite prepared to guarantee landowners' rights. In areas where there was no such gain to be made, the peasants were encouraged to appropriate the land and publicly degrade its former owners. Yet, whatever the arguments about Mao's methods, his massive personal contribution to the success of the CCP has never been seriously disputed. Against the odds, he had led the party to victory in civil war. Moreover, in the course of gaining that military success he had wrested the political initiative from Chiang and the GMD and stood poised to overthrow them.

However, what finally undermined the Nationalist government was not war or politics but economics. The military and political success of the Communists under Mao Zedong certainly played a vital part in determining their takeover in 1949, but it is arguable that the single most powerful reason for the failure of the GMD government was inflation. In 1937 the chronic but relatively mild rise in prices which China had experienced throughout the republican period began to climb uncontrollably.

The Inflationary Spiral, 1937-48	
notes issued (in millions of Chinese $)	price index
1937 2,060	100
1938 2,740	176
1939 4,770	323
1940 8,440	724
1941 15,810	1,980
1942 35,100	6,620
1943 75,400	22,800
1944 189,500	75,500
1945 1,031,900	249,100
1946 3,726,100	627,210
1947 33,188,500	10,340,000
1948 374,762,200	287,700,000

The soaring inflation had been caused initially by the Japanese occupation after 1937 of China's most prosperous and productive provinces. The government had tried to make up for the loss of revenue that this caused by borrowing heavily from abroad and by vastly increasing the issue of paper currency. The effect was a drastic fall in the value of money, a trend that was exacerbated by the huge military expenditure occasioned by the war. By 1945 the Nationalist government had raised an army of five million troops, an effort that accounted for 75 per cent of its expenditure. The government was in the impossible position of attempting to pay its escalating domestic and foreign debts with money that was becoming increasingly worthless. The rate of inflation reached astronomical heights after 1945. The Nationalist regime was helpless in the face of it. By 1949 China's monetary system had collapsed, the government was discredited, and the people of Nationalist China were demoralised. Even had the Nationalists not been defeated in civil war and driven from the mainland it is difficult to see how Chiang Kaishek and the GMD could have continued to hold power in China.

Studying 'Civil Strife in China, 1900-49'

The two chapters on China's domestic history can be conveniently broken down into five main sections: 1. The fall of the Manchu empire; 2. The warlord era; 3. The CCP in the Jiangxi and Yanan periods; 4. The Nationalists in power, 1935-45; 5. The Communist triumph in 1949. Each of these themes raises questions which are central to an examination of the internal conflicts in China.

1. The fall of the Manchu empire

Key question: How revolutionary was the Chinese revolution of 1911?

This question calls for a reading of Chapter 1 and the first section of Chapter 2.

Points to consider: Obviously the rising of 1911 is the central issue, but to understand that event it is necessary to examine the preceding decade. The imperial government's humiliating defeat in the Boxer Rising and the failure of its reform programme effectively destroyed any possibility of the Manchus leading a genuinely modernising movement. The attempts of Cixi and her successor, the Prince Regent, to preserve the monarchy proved unavailing. The fact was that the economic and social changes that had taken place in China since the 1840s had made the imperial system obsolete. This, rather than the strength of Sun Yatsen and the republicans explains why China was ripe for revolution by 1911. The mutiny of the Double Tenth at Wuhan was the occasion not the cause of the Manchu collapse. The dynasty could not long delay its abdication once it had been deserted by its natural supporters, the upper ranks of the army.

The revolution, therefore, was not the work of republican

```
┌─────────────────────────────────────────────────┐
│  The Struggle for Leadership of the Revolution    │
└─────────────────────────────────────────────────┘
```

GMD   CCP

the encirclement campaigns

the Long March, 1934-5

the Xian Incident, 1936
the 2nd United Front

the Years at Yanan, 1936-45
the Gospel from Yanan

Nationalist China, 1937-45
China's Destiny

Mao's Rectification Campaign
|
The Civil War, 1945-9
|
'the battle for the hearts of the people'

```
┌─────────────────────────────────────────────────┐
│     Reasons for Communist Victory in 1949         │
└─────────────────────────────────────────────────┘
```

Guomindang   Communists
| |
corruption   pro-peasant policies
factionalism   nationalism
detachment from China's real needs   intense dedication
dependence on foreign aid   high morale
inflation   Mao's leadership
economic failures   Mao's ruthlessness
coercive methods   superior strategy
failure to achieve the 3 Principles

Summary - Civil Strife in China, 1934-49

revolutionaries, though they obviously stood to gain from it. It was essentially a military affair. The radicals who joined in after the Double Tenth did so on the terms dictated by the military, who remained in charge of events. Equally significant was the inability of the central government to re-impose itself on the rebellious provinces, a failure that marked a victory for traditional Chinese regionalism. Indeed, the revolution of 1911-12 was very much a traditional affair, not a social but a palace revolution, with the mandate of heaven being handed on to the new Republic. Subsequent events, with parliamentarianism and democracy failing to take root, were to reveal how limited the changes brought about by the revolution had been. The strength of Chinese conservatism prevented the upheavals of 1911-12 from producing a total break in Chinese tradition.

2. The warlord era

Key question: Did the warlord era advance or retard the Chinese revolution?

The essential reading here is section 3 of Chapter 2. It would also be worthwhile to consult sections 2 and 3 in the Introduction.

Points to consider: This question requires a definition of the character and purpose of the 1911 revolution as well as a knowledge of the warlord period itself. If the Chinese revolution is defined as a movement aiming at greater national awareness and closer national integration, then the warlord period presented clear obstacles. The failure of the Chinese Republic after 1916 to replace Manchu autocracy with effective central government allowed locally powerful individuals to take over the regions. This fragmentation was an obvious check on the process towards national cohesion. However, despite the warlords, a strong residual nationalism remained, as witnessed by the 4 May Movement. Indeed, this movement was as much a reaction against the power of the warlords as against the presence of the foreign imperialists. The two main revolutionary parties, the CCP and the GMD, were both inspired by a hatred of warlordism. The United Front which they came together to form took as its most important task the destruction of the warlords.

While it is true, therefore, that disunity is the defining term for the warlord years, that very disunity intensified the bitterness of all Chinese nationalists and gave direction and focus to a revolutionary movement that might otherwise have weakened itself in inter-party disputes and local rivalries. Consciousness of the ills the nation was suffering under warlordism proved a powerful stimulus to China's cultural renaissance, whose high point coincided with the worst years of warlord oppression. The affronts to national pride perpetrated by warlords and foreign exploiters gave the Chinese people a collective sense of grievance. It was this that eventually checked the disruptive tendencies in republican China by providing a cause around which the Chinese could unite.

Although the GMD-CCP alliance broke down in the late 1920s, it had by then achieved its initial purpose of providing a successful anti-warlord combination. The initial effect of warlord rule had been to increase the fragmentation of China. Yet in the end this was more than counterbalanced by the stimulus that the period gave to China's sense of national identity.

3. The CCP in the Jiangxi and Yanan periods

Key question: How effectively did Mao Zedong adapt Marxist theory to Chinese conditions during the Jiangxi and Yanan years?

Sections 1, 2 and 4 of this chapter are the essential reading for this theme; reference should also be made to sections 4, 5 and 6 of Chapter 6, dealing with the Soviet Union.

Points to consider: Mao's relations with Stalin and the Comintern from the White Terror onwards convinced him that Soviet advice was unreliable. He concluded that if the CCP was to succeed it would be by in its own efforts, following its own interpretation of how Marxism could be best applied in China. Mao was unimpressed by the Comintern's insistence on urban-based revolution. At Jiangxi and Yanan he developed the concept of China's revolution as essentially a peasant-based movement. There was no need to wait for the growth of an industrial proletariat; the peasants would become the agents of genuine revolution. This re-ordering of the dialectical process involved Mao in a long-running battle with the hard-liners within the CCP who remained loyal to Moscow.

In the course of winning this struggle Mao established an ascendancy over his opponents similar to that achieved by Stalin in the USSR. As in the Soviet Union, so in Communist China, there emerged a powerful leader who was looked upon as the embodiment of revolutionary correctness. This enabled Mao to impose his interpretations upon the CCP. Mao's 'new democracy' was essentially authoritarian. The consequence was that Mao did not need to adapt to a pre-existing Marxist programme. Marxism, in effect, was what Mao said it was. It should be stressed that although Marx had stated the general principles of revolution, he had never defined how it would be achieved in practice. That was a task for later strategists. Lenin had applied his own interpretation to Russia. Mao would apply his to China. The essential question, therefore, is not how well Mao understood Marxist theory, but how well he understood the situation in China. His success by 1945 in establishing his dominance over the Party and in winning over the greater part of the peasantry to the CCP's cause testifies to the accuracy of his perception and judgement.

4. The Nationalists in power, 1935-45

Key question: Why did the Nationalist government prove incapable of consolidating its authority in China between 1935 and 1945?

The material relating to this theme is in section 4, but it would help to give a sense of perspective to refer also to sections 3 and 5.

Points to consider: Given the CCP's near extinction in 1935 and its struggle to survive during the Yanan years, it did indeed seem that the Nationalists had a decade in which to consolidate their hold of China. However, even at its strongest the GMD controlled only one third of the nation. Its power was restricted essentially to the south. It was also the case that, rather than having crushed the warlords, the Nationalists had been obliged to reach a compromise with them. Such factors, plus the presence of the Japanese occupying forces, were severe limitations on the GMD government's freedom of action. A further basic weakness of the GMD was that though its declared aim was to serve the Chinese population as a whole, it was in practice the representative only of particular interests. Chiang Kaishek's party was drawn from the small but powerful capitalist urban classes on whom it depended for its revenue; it never spoke for the great mass of rural China. Not being a genuinely popular party meant that it had to rely on coercion to maintain its power. This could work only for as long as it succeeded in remaining stronger than its opponents. By 1945 this was no longer the case.

During the decade in question the Nationalist government became enfeebled by uncontrolled inflation; the declining value of money made it increasingly difficult to finance the war effort against the Japanese and the CCP. It also left little in real terms to spend on industrial development and agrarian reform. China's greatest economic and social needs were thus ignored. Desperate for international capital, Chiang's government rather than freeing China from foreign domination increased its subservience. Moreover, despite Chiang's calls for moral reform he presided over an increasingly corrupt administration. By 1945 the 3 Principles of the People, which supposedly defined the Nationalists' political aims, were far from being realised. Democracy had not been achieved, social welfare had been largely neglected and China, notwithstanding its victory over Japan, was still far from being an independent nation. All the while the Nationalists were struggling to retain their grip, the Communists were expanding and consolidating their hold in the 'liberated areas' of northern China. In 1945 the Communists emerged from Yanan a stronger political and military force than the Nationalists.

5. The Communist triumph in 1949.

Key question: 'Ironically the defeat of the GMD by the CCP in 1949 was more a triumph of nationalism than of communism.' Discuss.

Sections 6 and 7 of this chapter are the most directly relevant, but an understanding of the material in the rest of the chapter is also required.

Points to consider: The civil war that was renewed in China after the defeat of Japan quickly revealed how little real support the GMD had in the country at large. Arguably it was only continued American support that enabled Chiang's government to remain in power. Chiang's failure to wrest the control of northern China from the Communists proved to be the beginning of the end for the GMD. Despite a superiority in troops and resources, Chiang's forces were unable to match the Reds in morale and commitment.

There is a strong case for saying that the increasing number of military defeats suffered by the GMD between 1946 and 1949 merely confirmed that Mao Zedong's pro-peasant policies during the Yanan years, had already 'won the hearts of the people'. Against the GMD's corruption, economic mismanagement, disregard of China's real needs, and continued subservience to the West, the CCP could boast an active sympathy with the masses of the Chinese peasantry and deep desire to save China from humiliation at the hands of outside enemies. Indeed, it was the CCP not the Nationalists who appeared to be fulfilling the 3 Principles of the People. The furtherance of democracy, social welfare and Chinese independence were not GMD but CCP achievements. The record of the Communists' rallying of all Chinese of good will in resistance to Japan further suggested that it was the CCP not the GMD who were the genuine nationalists. In addition, Mao's party had united a large part of the nation, and in their 'liberated areas' had introduced land reforms and political structures in which the local population felt they could directly participate. These successes were seen by their beneficiaries not in a political but social context. The simple fact was that life was better under the CCP than the GMD. This was in large part a product of Mao Zedong's shrewdness in playing down the party's political, class-war, objectives and emphasising its commitment to the regeneration of China as a nation. Chinese Communism was Chinese first and Communist second.

Source analysis - *'Civil Strife in China, 1900-49'*

There is a formula in document analysis that, when followed, guards against omitting any essential points. According to this formula, extracts are examined under three main headings: 1 - context, 2 - meaning, 3 - significance. Comments under 1 should place the piece in its immediate setting and background, describing where and when the source was written or appeared. 2 involves explaining the meaning and, where appropriate, the purpose of the text. It is in this section that particularly significant or difficult terms should be defined. Heading 3 provides the opportunity to expand upon the meaning of the source, putting it in its wider context and explaining how it relates to larger themes. The source analysis found in the study guides adopts this approach.

The following is an analysis of three separate but related documents concerning the key issue of Mao Zedong's organisation of the peasant movement. These appear on pages 39, 42 and 49.

1 - Context

The first extract dates from the 1920s at the time Mao had begun to challenge the Comintern's line in regard to the Chinese revolution. The second is Mao's assessment of the Long March, written shortly after the marchers had arrived in Yanan in 1935. The third is a set of instructions of the type first issued to Mao's troops during the Jiangxi period and repeated in various forms during the Yanan years.

2 - Meaning

In the first extract Mao describes the huge potential for revolution residing in the teeming Chinese peasantry. He foresees them as the irresistible force that will free China by breaking the grip of warlords and imperialists. In assessing the achievements of the Long March, Mao uses an extended agricultural metaphor. He celebrates the successful defiance of Chiang Kaishek's annihilation campaign as having sown the seeds of rural revolution throughout China. The key reference is in the first line where Mao summarises the essential characteristics of the March: it has proved to be 'a manifesto, an agitation corps, a seeding machine'. The third extract details the behaviour Mao requires of the Red Army in its treatment of the population of the areas it controls. The rules show an awareness of the brutality which armies had traditionally meted out to the peasants. Consideration, respect and honesty are to govern the troops' relations with the people. What Mao is defining is a set of common courtesies which will show the peasants that the Red Army truly understands the basic anxieties and needs of the Chinese people.

3 - Significance

Collectively what the three sources represent is Mao's recognition of the key role that the peasants are to play in the development of the Chinese revolution. The first extract unambiguously invokes the peasantry as the source of real revolution. Sheer peasant numbers make them the arbiters of Chinese politics. This marks the break between Mao Zedong and the Comintern that was to lead to decades of Sino-Soviet estrangement. By the late 1920s Mao has resolved that, regardless of Soviet orthodoxy with its insistence on proletarian uprising, the Chinese revolution will be a peasant affair. It follows that the CCP must educate the peasants into understanding their revolutionary role. An essential first step towards this is for the Red Army to make itself accepted as the peasants' natural ally. Mao believes that the Long March provided the Communists with an ideal situation in which to advance that message. The success of the March in politicising the peasantry is thus to be explained by reference to the sensitivity the Reds showed towards peasant needs. This is illustrated by the code of behaviour that Mao laid down for the Red Army in its dealings with the localities. It was all part of his larger campaign for defeating the GMD by 'winning the hearts of the people'. The extracts are key examples, therefore, of the essentially practical nature of Mao Zedong's approach to the organising of a mass party among the Chinese peasants.

CHAPTER 4

China and the West

1 Introduction

Imperialism is a highly controversial topic. There are many conflicting views about the motivation behind it and the effects it produced. However, notwithstanding their differences of opinion over its virtues or failings, historians are now broadly agreed that imperialism was never a single movement with a single purpose. Its components do not add up to a neat whole. Each area needs to be studied on its own terms in order to assess the impact that colonialism had upon it. In studying the character of imperialism as it operated in modern China, what emerges is a relationship between the West and the Chinese of exploiter and exploited. The story that is traced in the following chapter is broadly a record of how the Western powers sought to use China for their own ends. During the half century after 1900 opportunities occurred for the West to stabilise its relations with China on the basis of mutual respect and benefit; these were not taken. There is a complementary theme - the difficulty the Chinese had in developing sufficient unity of purpose to mount an effective national resistance movement against Western dominance.

The defeat of China in the Sino-Japanese war in 1895 (see page 21) had prompted a number of Western powers to tighten their hold on China. In what is often referred to as the 'scramble for concessions', France, Britain, Russia and Germany forced the Chinese to enter into a further series of 'unequal treaties', in which the European nations considerably extended their territorial and commercial interests in China. One particularly notable example of this occurred in 1898 when Britain negotiated a 99-year leasehold on the port of Kowloon. There seemed to be a real possibility that China might suffer the same fate as Africa, which was currently being carved up between the European imperial powers in the 'Scramble for Africa' (1870-1914). In 1904, a British force, having marched into the north-western border province of Tibet, obliged the Manchu government to recognise Tibetan independence. This in effect was an acknowledgement of Britain's control of the region, which in an earlier century the Qing dynasty had taken great pride in incorporating into China. The Russians in a similar move at this time demanded that China recognise their influence in Outer Mongolia. As the Manchu power weakened in the first decade of the century the ability of the West to direct Chinese affairs increased.

What prevented China's complete fragmentation was the attitude of the USA, which had recently entered the world stage. Despite its anti-colonial tradition, America had begun to develop its own brand of imperialism, as evident at the end of the century in its military adventures in Cuba and the Philippines. The USA had played no part in the scramble for Africa, but it was determined to assert itself in the Pacific region. It adopted a policy for preventing the same subdivision of China as had occurred in Africa. Through its Secretary of State, John Hay, the USA in 1899 warned off the other imperial powers. In diplomatic but unambiguous terms, Hay informed them that America was not prepared to see China's economy fall under their control. No country was entitled to force the Chinese to grant it preferential tariffs; China must be left free to develop its trade and commerce with whom it chose. Although few of the powers were happy with this 'open door' doctrine, none was prepared at this stage to challenge the USA directly over it.

Chinese protests against Western domination were frequent but largely ineffectual since they lacked leadership and co-ordination. It is true that the Manchus supported the Boxers in 1900 but the Chinese government was never sufficiently consistent in its opposition to foreign influence to lead a genuinely anti-Western movement. Sporadic machine breaking and sabotage of industrial plant clearly expressed the Chinese workers' objection to foreign control but did little to threaten it. In 1905 a boycott of American goods was organised as a protest against the adoption of immigration laws in the USA which specifically discriminated against the Chinese. Although interesting as an example of Chinese resentment, the incident remained merely one of a rash of unco-ordinated reactions. What undermined attempts to develop an effective anti-foreigner movement was the inescapable fact that large numbers of Chinese had come to depend for their livelihood on the Western presence. This was particularly evident in the major cities such as Beijing, Guangzhou and Shanghai, where thousands of Chinese workers were employed by foreign companies or in the international concessions. Western favours could not to be rejected out of hand. Foreign capital was necessary for Chinese regeneration. It was the GMD's need of finance that made Sun Yatsen, and to an even greater extent Chiang Kaishek, compromise with the Western occupiers.

2 Western Attitudes towards China

The indifference with which so many Western expatriates treated the Chinese and their culture arose from a feeling of innate superiority. The Western nationals who lived in China belonged to one of three broad categories: diplomatic staff, foreign-company personnel and religious missionaries. All three groups grew considerably in number during the period of the scramble for concessions. With few exceptions they had one of two attitudes towards the Chinese; they either despised or patronised them. This can be gauged from the following extracts. Writing in 1906, Fr.Richard, a French Jesuit priest, made little effort to disguise his distaste for those he was trying to convert to Christianity. He described his idea of the typical Chinese:

1 Proud and conceited with his own superiority, he hates foreigners
  because their excellence is conspicuous. He is not particularly
  clean in his person, habits or surroundings and is rather indifferent
  about smells and noises. He has no lofty ideal of life, and is
5 deficient especially in the higher moral qualities: sense of duty,
  trustworthiness, sacrifice for the general welfare, public spirit,
  enthusiasm and active courage in danger.

A Protestant missionary was equally forthright in his comment on the
incapacity of the Chinese educated classes to adjust to Western
dominance:

1 It is impossible not to displease them. To preach is to insult them,
  for in the very act you assume the position of a teacher. To publish
  a book on religion or science is to insult them, for in doing that you
  take for granted that China is not the depository of all truth and
5 knowledge. To propound progress is to insult them, for therein
  you intimate that China has not reached the very acme of
  civilisation, and that you stand on a higher platform than they.

It was in reaction to such dismissive attitudes that numbers of Chinese
participated in the Boxer Rising of 1900 against the 'foreign devils', with
Christian missionaries as a particular target. What is especially
instructive about the Rising is that the atrocities perpetrated by the
Boxers were deliberately matched by the international army drawn from
the concession areas to crush it. The German Field-Marshal,
Waldersee, who was appointed Commander of the multi-national force,
received this instruction from Kaiser William II:

1 Just as the Huns a thousand years ago, under the leadership of
  Attila, gained a reputation by virtue of which they still live in
  historical tradition, so may the name of Germany become known
  in such a manner in China, that no Chinese will ever again dare to
5 look askance at a German.

Waldersee was only too eager to obey. In suppressing the Boxers, his
forces deliberately humiliated and degraded the population of the areas
through which they passed. The systematic rape and killing of civilians
and the looting and destruction of premises became the order of the day.
     An important explanation for the relative ease with which the
Western powers and Japan overcame the Boxers was the readiness of
local provincial and military leaders to co-operate with the international
army. They ignored the Beijing government's call for a united Chinese
resistance and agreed instead to act as protectors of the foreign nationals
in China. Compromises such as these were symptomatic of China's
besetting weakness in its relations with the West; too many Chinese had

a vested interest in the maintenance of Western domination of their country. The West's awareness of this served to confirm its low estimation of the Chinese. Even the fall of the Manchus and the creation of the Republic did little to alter the view of Westerners, whose prevailing scepticism regarding China's ability to modernise was typified in the response of the London *Times* to the 1911 revolution.

1 Some of those who know China best cannot but doubt whether a
  form of government so utterly alien to Oriental conceptions and to
  Oriental traditions as a Republic can be suddenly substituted for a
  monarchy in a nation of four hundred millions of men, whom
5 Kings with semi-divine attributes have ruled since the dim twilight
  of history.

3 The West's Economic Relationship with China

It is doubtful that the Western powers had a real wish to see China modernise. Although in their public statements they invariably expressed the hope that China would grow into a strong industrial nation, it was very much in their commercial interest for it to remain relatively weak. The obvious attraction of China for Western industrialists was that it provided a source of cheap labour and materials. As a result, the international concession areas and treaty ports witnessed a marked increase in factory development and industrial activity in the first decade of the century. The favourable tariff rates that the West had extracted from the Chinese under the unequal treaties, considered together with low wage and production costs, made China an especially inviting proposition for Western entrepreneurs. Minimal outlay and high returns formed the ideal economic equation. Western companies monopolised the industrial ventures. Even where Chinese companies appeared to have the responsibility for the enterprise, Western financiers invariably demanded a controlling voice in the running of the business.

Western financial and banking interests calculated that the Chinese market offered rich returns. In one sense this brought advantages to the Chinese; the inflow of foreign investment increased the capital stock available to them. But China's relative economic weakness meant that it was always on the wrong end of the bargain in its dealings with the West. Loans were negotiated in favour of the Western financiers advancing them, rather than the Chinese recipients. It was an extension of the unequal treaties. China could do little about this. It wished to modernise its economy by means of industrial development, but industrialisation required access to large sources of capital. There was no way China could raise the sums necessary other then by borrowing from abroad.

This was particularly evident in the major industrial growth area, the railways. In the first decade of the century, China experienced a major expansion of its railroads and rolling stock. It was a nationwide development that promised to bring prosperity to most regions of China. This raised a political problem for the Manchus. If significant amounts of capital went to the localities, this would result in local control of the provincial railways, a prospect that was viewed by Beijing as a dangerous challenge to its central authority. To wrest control of China's communication system from the provincial companies, the imperial government undertook what amounted to a railway nationalisation programme, the costs of which were to be met by borrowing from the West. Thus the Manchus were seeking to keep central control at the cost of increased international indebtedness.

This burden of debt was a crippling legacy that the new regime inherited in 1912. The desperate need for capital, which had been such a prominent feature of imperial China, remained equally pressing under the Republic. It was also still the case that the only substantial means of acquiring finance was by borrowing. In order to raise essential loans, the Republic under Yuan Shikai had to accept the dictates of a six-member international Banking Commission which had been originally set up in 1911 during the last days of the Qing dynasty. The USA had been instrumental in the formation of the Commission as part of its 'dollar diplomacy', a modification of the 'open door' doctrine; to further US financial interests, President Taft had personally contacted the Chinese government in 1909 to urge them to accept increased American investment. The Commission eventually offered a loan of $100 million but on terms that required China to nominate its future tax revenues as collateral and to place the administration of Chinese finances in the hands of foreign controllers. Among other concessions wrung from the republican government were its recognition of Britain's control of Tibet and Russia's of Outer Mongolia. It was clear that Yuan's successful negotiation of the loan had been achieved only at the price of a further loss of Chinese independence. Equally significant was Japan's use of its newly-won influence with the Western powers to insist that it be included as one of the Commission's members. This was further proof both of Japan's superiority over China and of the West's acceptance of this as a basic fact of international relations.

In describing the manner in which Western capitalism exploited the situation in China, it has to be said that not all Chinese were reluctant to be exploited. Many were prepared to tolerate the poor wages and conditions because the Chinese domestic economy had nothing better to offer them. The abuse of workers was not something brought by the West. It was traditional in China. The eagerness of peasants to leave the land and work in Western-owned factories indicated how precarious and grim their previous life had been. The same was true of locally owned industries. Chinese bosses did not have a reputation for the humane treatment of their employees. China's small-scale domestic industries had been run as sweatshops of the most oppressive kind.

Moreover, the expansion of Western enterprise offered greatly increased work prospects for the Chinese. This was especially true for women, who now had the opportunity to supplement the meagre family income. A further positive effect was that Western industrial expansion encouraged the growth of Chinese business. China was introduced to the arts of industrial management and training. This educative process was increased by the experience of those thousands of young Chinese who studied abroad. Their exposure to concepts which had become standard in the West, such as specialised training and applied technology, both fired and compromised their nationalism. They began to ask why Western advances had not been achieved in China. In answering their own question they became increasingly resentful, not simply of Western supremacy but of their own national traditions and forms of government which inhibited Chinese progress. Much as they might hate the West, they judged that it was only by a Western path that they could achieve their goals. This was evident in the rush to adopt Western styles that followed the 1911 revolution. A Canadian resident in Beijing observed:

1 I was away from 1910 to 1912 ... Going away in 1910, we went away from an imperialist China that was advancing quite nicely. But it was 'Chinese' with still the long pigtail, the wide-sleeved coat and the high shoes with the thick felt soles for the mandarin.
5 Coming back you had this craziest impact of western fashions. It was very modern to wear a felt fedora hat. These were made in China. There wasn't a good hat business, but they did their best, and they certainly put out a hodge-podge of fedora hats which you creased down the middle. The other mark of being an absolutely
10 modern Chinese was to wear long winter underwear during the winter. But how would people know you had the underwear if you wore it inside? So they wore it outside. It was the craziest thing to see literally dozens of men, and these were the snobs of the city, who wore their long-johns outside, and perhaps an umbrella in his
15 hand - that also was a mark of status - and a felt fedora hat. This lasted four or five years ...

Also, for those few years, everything that was traditionally Chinese was looked down upon and everything from the West was marvellous. The day of the dollar watch; the day of the flashlight
20 coming in, the umbrella, the bicycle ... It became swank to say a few words of English. The local turned-on fellow would be very happy, instead of bowing to you, to say 'goodbye'.

This adulation of Western externals may appear quaint but it was a manifestation of something deeper, the desire to see China modernised. There is an arguable case for suggesting that had the West treated China with sympathy and tact at this stage the subsequent history of the Far East might have been substantially different. The eagerness among the Chinese to embrace Western ways was such that they may well have been willing to overlook past slights if the West had now been willing to deal with them on equal terms. But even had the Western nations been prepared to reverse their established policy of exploitation, the turn of world events prevented them from considering the China question except in terms of their own interests. The West's preoccupation first with the 1914-18 war and then with the onset of economic depression in the late 1920s diverted their attention away from China at a crucial stage in its development as a republic. The result was that the Chinese reformers felt betrayed. The Chinese revolution in 1911 and the creation of the Republic, events that were based ostensibly on Western democratic principles, had not brought the expected benefits. Nor was it simply a question of Western indifference. When the Western powers did turn their attention again towards China they appeared to be more exploitative than ever.

4 International Relations and China, 1900-20

A major shift in the relations between the international powers took place in the decade or so before 1914; it was a realignment that had profound repercussions for China. Following the war between Russia and Japan (1904-5), the two combatants sought to avoid further conflict by drawing together diplomatically. A series of negotiations culminated in 1912 with a formal Russo-Japanese agreement. The public part of this agreement spoke of the two countries' readiness to respect Chinese independence, but in a set of secret clauses Japan and Russia recognised each other's spheres of influence in the China region, specifically in Manchuria, Korea and Outer Mongolia.

In a parallel international adjustment in the West, Britain, France and Russia had also drawn closer to each other. The motive of the Western powers was essentially to offset the growing military power of Germany in Europe, but their understanding had important Far Eastern implications since Britain had already entered into an alliance with Japan in 1902, in which the two countries had promised not to challenge each other's naval power in that area. Now, by extension, Japan was brought closer to Britain's new allies. National interests were drawing countries together in a series of overlapping agreements. At no point was China consulted even though many of the treaties and agreements impinged very directly upon it. Despite formal recognition of its sovereign rights, China continued to have its particular interests largely ignored.

The USA was concerned that its expansion into the Pacific region would at some point conflict with Japanese interests. To lessen the likelihood of tension, the Americans adopted the prevailing pattern of entering into formal understandings. In 1908 Japan and the USA arrived at the Root-Takahira agreement in which the two nations recognised each other's rights in the Far East and committed themselves to the continuance of the open door policy in China. For America's part, the agreement was a means of persuading the Japanese to accept the tight restriction on Asian immigration into the USA, which it had recently imposed.

What Japan had effectively done in the first fifteen years of the century was to win the support of the Western powers in its dealings with China. This did not mean that the West had entirely lost its misgivings about the growth of Japanese strength but it did strongly suggest that China stood very low in Western estimation. How low became clear with the outbreak of war in Europe in 1914.

a) China and the First World War

Initially, the Allied powers - France, Russia and Britain - had urged China as well as Japan to declare war on Germany. However, Japan, worried that this might improve the international standing of the Chinese, persuaded the Beijing government to delay its entry. In addition, Japan obtained from the British a secret promise that they would not press for China's entry without first consulting Tokyo. Thus diplomatically fortified, Japan then seized the German territories in China, including Shandong province with its key port of Qingdao. At the time, the Japanese declared that these possessions would eventually be returned to China, but the emptiness of that promise became evident in 1915 when Japan's notorious 21 Demands threatened to reduce China to a Japanese vassal state (see page 96). The Chinese appealed to the Western powers for support but received only a muted response. The United States accepted that Japan's 'territorial contiguity' with China entitled it to the areas it had taken. Britain was disturbed by those Demands which were thought to give Japan too great an extension of naval power in the Far East, but, once it had obtained Japan's agreement to suspend those clauses indefinitely, it raised no objection to the 21 Demands in principle.

Britain's reluctance to take China's side at this point arose from its concern to avoid offending Japan as a major war ally. By 1915 it was becoming clear that the European war would be a protracted one. Britain and the Allies simply could not afford to risk losing Japan's support. However, it was this same reason, the mounting demands of the war effort, that led the Allies in 1917 to renew their appeal to China to join the hostilities against Germany. Up to that year the Chinese had maintained their neutrality. If the Chinese were to be persuaded to join the war they would have to be convinced that an Allied victory would guarantee their recovery of the disputed territories that Japan had seized.

The Americans played a key role at this juncture. Having themselves joined the war against Germany in 1917, they urged China to do the same. The USA suggested to the Chinese that if they fought for the Allies this would earn them a place at the postwar conference table where they would be in a position to claim their rights. Many Chinese, including Sun Yatsen and the GMD, remained unconvinced by this American analysis. Nevertheless, the Beijing government judged that the USA, which under Woodrow Wilson had entered the war avowedly 'to make the world safe for democracy', was more to be trusted than the European Allies. Strengthened by a substantial US loan, China formally declared war on Germany in August 1917.

This time Japan raised no objection, not because it had come to accept China's territorial rights but because it had already obtained formal commitments from the Western Allies that they would continue to recognise the priority of Japanese claims to German possessions in China. Britain, France, Russia and Italy had all secretly pledged themselves to support Japan in any postwar settlement. Moreover, the Chinese had already been betrayed from within. Duan Qirui, China's chief representative in the negotiations with the Western powers, had attempted to win Japanese backing so as to strengthen his position as head of the Beijing government in the uncertain period that followed Yuan Shikai's death. In return for Japanese loans and military aid, Duan agreed in secret talks that his government would fully recognise Japan's special privileges in China. This agreement was extended into a formal Sino-Japanese military alliance early in 1918. The official reason given for such military co-operation was that the Russo-German armistice on the Eastern Front in Europe, which had followed the Russian Revolution in October 1917, had created a situation 'which seems likely to threaten the peace and security of the Far East'. However, behind the words was Japan's wish to justify its invasion of Siberia, which had been launched as one of the anti-Bolshevik foreign interventions in the Russian civil war of 1918-20. Japan claimed to have special interests in Siberia that it was entitled to protect. At each stage in Sino-Japanese negotiations it was Japan's needs that determined their supposedly joint policies.

After entering the European war China played no direct role in the fighting, but its contribution to the Allied effort was far from insignificant. Over 150,000 Chinese labourers went to the Western Front where, in addition to working in munitions factories, they dug graves and maintained 90 miles of Anglo-French trenches. The Chinese believed that such endeavour should be rewarded by favourable attention being given to their claims in the postwar settlement.

b) China and the Versailles Treaty

The end of the 1914-18 war and the peace settlement that followed provided a perfect opportunity for the Allied victors to apply to China the principles of democracy and self-determination for which they professed to have fought. But these principles were honoured selectively not universally. No consideration was given by the Western powers to the abandoning of their special privileges or concession areas in China. In the redrawing of the map of the Far East the Western negotiators pointedly gave precedence to Japan, as they had promised to do in their secret wartime agreements. At the Versailles Conference the previous German treaty rights and possessions on the Chinese mainland were not restored to China but were granted instead to Japan. This was a direct negation of the commitment given to China to persuade it to enter the war in 1917.

China had every reason to feel outraged over its treatment. In no respect had it benefited from the supposed victory of democracy in Europe. The news that not only had the Western powers betrayed China at Versailles but that the Beijing leaders had colluded in their nation's humiliation produced the 4 May disturbances, the first stage of the national movement in China which stimulated the growth of China's two revolutionary parties, the GMD and the CCP. Significantly, both these parties resolved that only by removing Western influence could China begin to regenerate itself. For the Chinese Communists it was Marxism's character as an anti-Western, anti-imperialist ideology that gave it its special relevance and appeal, an appeal that was reinforced by Bolshevik Russia's declaration in 1919 that it was giving up all rights and privileges in China previously claimed by tsarist governments.

5 The Western Realignment over China, 1920-31

Despite the fierce nationalism of the 4 May Movement after 1919, the powers were not yet prepared to make any real concession to Chinese demands. This was apparent in an American proposal put forward in 1920 to extend Western financial control by the creation of an international banking consortium to direct China's financial affairs. However, on this occasion, the Chinese were unwilling to accept the proposal since they judged that the consortium, which would have included Japan as a member, would simply serve to strengthen the Japanese grip upon China that had been established by the 21 Demands and the Versailles settlement.

Japan was certainly the key factor in the Far East in the judgement of the Western powers. Believing that the various agreements they had made with Japan during the course of the 1914-18 war had altered the balance of power in the Far East, the powers convened an international conference at Washington. Britain was a prime mover in this. The British together with the French and the Dutch, the only imperialist nations in Europe to have survived the war with their Far Eastern empires intact, were worried by the growing strength of the Japanese. Britain's àim was to protect its Far Eastern commercial and strategic interests without losing the friendship of the USA or antagonising Japan. At the time it had proposed the financial consortium, the USA, in keeping with its anti-imperialist stance, had spoken of the need to replace the old colonialism with a new international balance in the Far East. Underlying that statement was an American anxiety about the extension of Japanese power in the Pacific region. The USA was as keen as the other powers to protect its own interests by an international agreement.

The Washington Conference was held between November 1921 and February 1922. It produced two treaties, dealing respectively with commercial and naval matters, and a nine-power agreement on China. In an apparent concession to China's financial needs, the commercial treaty allowed the Chinese to retain a far larger proportion of their tariff revenue than previously, but administrative control of the customs system remained in foreign hands. The naval treaty involved the abandoning of the Anglo-Japanese alliance of 1902, which the British now regarded as an encumbrance since it blocked the way to closer relations with the Americans, and its replacement by a four-power agreement between Britain, France, Japan and the USA. In return for the recognition of its supremacy in home waters, Japan accepted a limitation on its naval resources; its warship strength would be maintained at a ratio of 3:5:5 in relation to the British and American fleets.

The nine-power agreement, to which the Chinese were a party, acknowledged China's rights as a nation and referred to the need to end foreign extra-territoriality, but no moves were made to put these general principles into practical effect. The unequal treaties were not rescinded and so continued to determine the character of China's relations with the West. Later events were to show that the powers still regarded it as perfectly normal for them to deal unilaterally with China without any reference to international agreements. A tariff conference which was convened in 1925 to give effect to the 1922 commercial treaty broke up with nothing settled.

It is argued by some historians that just as the 1919 peace settlement had provided an occasion when the West could have begun to end its exploitation of China, so, too, the Washington Conference gave the powers the chance to create a new order in the Far East in which the justice of Chinese claims to genuine national independence could have been internationally recognised. But the familiar story continued; despite their formal acknowledgement of China's sovereignty, the powers continued to behave in practice with little regard for Chinese national aspirations.

However, other writers point to the problems that stood in the way of the West's achieving an acceptable settlement of the China question. Major difficulties were the unstable internal condition of China and the weakness of its central government. The authority that the Beijing government struggled to exercise was restricted to the north of the country. From its base at Guangzhou, the GMD claimed to be the nation's legitimate government and mocked Beijing's ineffectiveness and incompetence. It was certainly true that the Beijing government, insolvent and unrepresentative of the nation as a whole, had played a feeble role at the Washington Conference. The GMD-CCP United Front, asserting that it now spoke for the real China, totally rejected the treaties and agreements to which Beijing had been a party. The Communists and the Nationalists both condemned the Washington Conference as being simply a front for further Western imperialist aggrandisement in China.

The fragmentation of the power structure in China in the 1920s certainly created difficulties for the West. With the official republican government in constant conflict with warlords, Nationalists and Communists, it was not easy for the Western nations to decide with which clique they should negotiate. This became particularly problematic at the time of the Northern Expedition and the White Terror between 1926 and 1928. The Western powers were initially unsure whether to support the Nationalists in their attack upon the warlords and the Communists. Their prime concern was naturally to protect their own people and interests in the concession areas. When Chiang Kaishek promised that his GMD forces would safeguard foreign personnel and property in China and maintain law and order, Britain and the USA began the practice of regarding him as the legitimate leader of China with whom it was expedient to deal. Yet this did not betoken any great understanding between the British and the Americans over China. Indeed, until they became wartime allies in 1941, the USA remained resentful of Britain as an imperial power.

There is a further crucial consideration. In spite of the superficial amity between the powers at the Washington Conference, the 1920s were a period during which the Japanese grew steadily more convinced that the USA was deliberately seeking their commercial ruin by closing its markets to their goods. To avoid the economic collapse that the Americans were trying to engineer, Japan resolved to compensate itself by appropriating such Chinese territory and resources as were necessary. The threat which this represented to China came to overshadow all its domestic and foreign affairs. The agreements that the international powers had previously reached over the Far Eastern question were of little relevance in the face of Japan's aggressive expansionism. From 1922 until 1945 it was Japanese not Western imperialism that shaped China's destiny. This is not to deny the importance of internal political developments in China or of the West's involvement in them, but it is to emphasise that those developments took the form they did largely in response to the growing menace of Japan.

6 The West and the Sino-Japanese Conflict, 1931-41

The aggressive nature of Japan's designs on China became unmistakable with the occupation of Manchuria in 1931. Here appeared to be another moment when the Western powers could have defended Chinese interests by acting together in joint resistance to Japanese expansionism in the Far East. But, notwithstanding much talk among the Western nations about the need for collective security, they took no steps to turn talk into action. Preoccupation with their own problems was one obvious reason why they did not. At this stage the reluctance of the powers to become involved in the Sino-Japanese issue had less to do with China than with a concern for their own economic crises. The severe depression that began in the Western world in 1929 and lasted for a decade made the nations inward looking and reluctant to engage in those foreign affairs which they judged did not directly involve them. Progressive internationalism could make little headway in such an atmosphere.

a) The League of Nations and China

Even when Japan extended its Manchurian occupation into a full-scale attack on China in 1937, the Western powers were still unwilling to act. The League of Nations, set up in 1919 as an international forum for resolving international disputes, did formally condemn Japanese aggression, but the key feature of the League at this juncture was its inability to enforce its will. Despite the hopes invested in it by those who still believed in collective security, the League lacked the membership of the key players in international affairs. The USA was never a member and, although the USSR joined in 1934, the withdrawal of both Japan and Germany in the 1930s cancelled out that gain. Moreover, whenever individual nations considered the League to be acting in a way inimical to their interests, they declined to co-operate with it or respect its resolutions. The League had no effective mechanism for obliging its member states to conform to its collective decisions. More importantly, it had no military powers. When confronted by cases of aggression by stronger nations against weaker, the League's only means of applying pressure was to impose economic sanctions on the wrong-doer. To be effective these needed time to work and the genuine commitment of the states imposing them. The record shows that in two major cases, the Italian conquest of Ethiopia and the Japanese occupation of China, the attempts of the League of Nations to apply sanctions against the aggressors were largely nullified by the failure of so many member states to co-operate.

The weakness of the League of Nations did not denote a lack of international interest in the Sino-Japanese conflict. Newsreels carried grim pictures of Japanese atrocities in China into cinemas worldwide.

Indeed, Western perceptions of the horror of modern warfare were often drawn from the scenes of the Japanese bombing of Chinese civilians as depicted in these films. Yet this did not create any real determination on the part of the international community to become involved in the struggle. The League continued to criticise Japanese excesses, but its protestations were little more than gestures. The Americans similarly condemned Japan for its inhumanity, but although individual volunteers, such as General Chennault and his team of 'flying tigers', fought for the Chinese, the USA as a nation was not prepared before 1941 to become directly engaged in the struggle.

Europe was no more willing than the USA to respond actively. France and Britain individually expressed anger at Japan's treatment of the Chinese, but, apart from taking extra precautions to safeguard their territorial and strategic interests in the region, they made no positive move to resist Japan. It is true that they recognised and paid verbal tributes to Chiang Kaishek as leader of the Chinese people in their resistance to the aggressor, but right up to the time of Pearl Harbor Western commercial links with Japan were maintained. In the case of the Western oil companies, their volume of trade with Japan actually increased between 1937 and 1941 as they sought to cash in on Japan's growing military need for fuel.

As for the Axis powers, Germany and Italy, Japan's humiliation of China earned their approval. As fascist states, they looked upon Japan as an oriental version of themselves. Such convergence of feeling became formalised with the creation in 1936 of the Anti-Comintern Pact between Germany, Italy and Japan. Germany was naturally cautious in regard to Japanese expansion since it still hankered after its former possessions in the Far East. But on the broader political issues Japan and Germany now had much in common. The result was that Germany was prepared to give Japan a free hand in its dealings with China.

As the League of Nations' protests had shown, the behaviour of the Japanese had created worldwide concern, but there was little possibility of this being turned into a collective response. International relations in the period 1919-39 afford few examples of successful co-operation between nations. National rivalries and suspicions prevented it. The world's strongest power, the USA, had withdrawn behind its tariff wall and was reluctant to become involved in events taking place beyond its shores. Its failure to follow up the opportunity for international co-operation provided by the Washington Conference meant that it tended to regard the Sino-Japanese question in a very restricted way. Part of the reason for this was the United States' professed distaste for imperialism, particularly the British variety. Japanese strength in the Far East, although obviously a development that needed monitoring lest it should threaten American Pacific interests, did provide a balance against the supposed might of the British Empire. Given such an attitude, the chances of an Anglo-American accord over Japan were extremely remote. It required Japan's attack upon Pearl Harbor in 1941 to push Britain and America into alliance and into undertaking the defence of China.

It was for these reasons that in the initial stages of the Sino-Japanese War, 1937-41, China stood alone. The western powers were not prepared to abandon their detachment from oriental affairs sufficiently to become directly involved on the China front. Neither the USA nor Britain, the two powers with the closest involvement in the Far East, was prepared to interfere at this stage. Britain was, of course, anxious over its territories in that region, but hoped that the Washington agreements and legacy of its previous alliance with Japan would hold good. The USA, still clinging to its isolationism, saw no reason for involvement.

7 China and the Second World War, 1941-5

The indifference of the West to the fate of China changed dramatically in December 1941. Japan's attack on the US Pacific fleet at Pearl Harbor, followed soon after by Germany's declaration of war against the USA, immediately brought America into the conflict. What had been an essentially Chinese affair was now a vital part of the much larger Second World War. From that time on, China was seen by the Allies as vital to the defeat of Japan. China would be sent huge quantities of supplies in an Allied effort to turn it into a base of operations. By 1945, the US had invested over $1 billion in China. The status that China now enjoyed among the Allies led Britain and the USA in 1942 to abandon most of the unequal treaties which had plagued China's relations with the West for so long. In addition, the international concession areas and the principle of extra-territoriality were abandoned. It is unthinkable that these gains would have been achieved but for the extraordinary impact that the Second World War had upon China's relations with the Western powers. Chiang Kaishek's personal position was further enhanced when his attendance at the Cairo Conference in 1943 appeared to elevate him to the rank of international statesman alongside Churchill and Roosevelt. It was at Cairo that Chiang was given the Allies' promise that when final victory came China would recover all the territories and privileges that Japan had taken from it since 1895.

However, contrary to appearances, Britain was unhappy about the new diplomatic status accorded to China and Chiang Kaishek. It was only at Roosevelt's insistence that Churchill had agreed to it. In private, Churchill expressed incredulity at the notion of recognising China as being on a par with the major Allies:

1 It is quite untrue to say that China is a world power equal to Britain, the United States or Russia ... The idea that China is going to have a say in the affairs of Europe 'other than ceremonial', or

that China should be rated for European purposes above France or
5 Poland or Austria-Hungary, or above even the smallest but
ancient, historic and glorious States like Holland, Belgium, Greece
and Yugoslavia - has only to be stated to be dismissed.

There is a strong revisionist school of thought that believes the USA
deliberately cultivated China at this time in order to have a grateful Far
Eastern ally, willing to do its bidding at the end of the war. Events in
1945 do seem to bear this out. At the Yalta Conference, to which China
was not invited, the USA and Britain secretly obtained Russia's
commitment to enter the Pacific war at an appropriate future date. As
part of the enticement, Russia was offered the restoration of all the
territories it had lost in the Russo-Japanese war in 1905. Since this
included significant parts of Manchuria and Mongolia, it meant that the
promise made to China at Cairo two years earlier of full restitution of its
territories could not be kept. That the USA was able subsequently to
persuade Nationalist China to accept this without serious demur, and in
addition to sign 'a treaty of friendship' with the USSR in August 1945,
proved that the USA had indeed created a malleable ally. All this
suggested that China's claim to world status had been wildly inflated.
The reality was that the international reputation of Chiang and of China
had depended on the goodwill of the USA.

Yet for Chiang Kaishek the importance of having America's
recognition was not international but domestic. The material and
diplomatic support of the USA furnished the means for realising the
dream that had sustained him ever since the Japanese invasion of China
in 1937; namely, that if the USA could be persuaded to enter the
military struggle in the Far East this would guarantee not simply the
defeat of Japan but also the destruction of his Communist enemies
within. Had the war not ended in the dramatic and unforeseen way that
it did with the atomic bombing of the Japanese mainland, Chiang's
beliefs might well have been borne out. But the Japanese surrender in
1945, which made the anticipated large-scale American troop landings
in China unnecessary, left the job half done as far as Chiang was
concerned. The Reds would not now be crushed by the might of the
USA. Although the Americans continued to provide diplomatic and
material support for Chiang Kaishek throughout the four years of the
GMD-CCP civil war, this was never enough to stem what became a Red
tide. What was proved first by the survival of the Communists and then
by their eventual victory in 1949 was that both Chiang and the USA had
failed to understand the remarkable political and social revolution that
Mao Zedong had wrought in China during the Yanan years.

Despite its long association with China, the USA's major Western
ally, Britain, was no closer to grasping the reality of Chinese internal
politics. How badly it failed to appreciate the real balance of power
between the CCP and the GMD was evident in a representative piece in

The *Observer* of August 1945, concerning the Sino-Soviet Friendship Treaty:

1 The Chinese Communists can expect neither sympathy nor support from Moscow. This means, in effect, that they will be unable to challenge the authority of Chungking. The Communist administration in North China has brought a number of
5 advantages to the peasants and undoubtedly makes a great appeal to them, but it has little to offer to the great commercial centres like Shanghai, or even Nanking. Moreover, the claim of its leaders to represent some 90 million Chinese is a gross exaggeration ...

If the Chinese Communists secure, as they are now hoping to
10 do, substantial quantities of Japanese arms, they may still be able to give a good deal of trouble to the Chungking Government. But without Russian assistance this could hardly last very long. Moreover, public opinion in China will be strongly averse from further war, especially civil war. At the same time, the moral and
15 political atmosphere has been lightened by victory over the Japanese, by the Treaty with Russia, and by the increasingly progressive attitude adopted by Chiang's Government.

8 China and the USA

When the Americans, anxious after Pearl Harbor to use China principally as a means of defeating Japan, examined the Chinese political spectrum they necessarily concentrated on those features likely to give them the easiest path to an anti-Japanese combination. Chiang Kaishek, who since the remarkable events of 1936-7 had been acknowledged as the leader of China, was the obvious person with whom to liaise. All Chiang's public pronouncements from 1937 onwards were delivered with the intention of convincing the Western world that he was not merely to be trusted but that he was indeed the only real hope of a successful unifying of the Chinese war effort against Japan.

Arguably, the USA grasped the importance and strength of the Chinese Communists only after it was too late. In their desperation to defeat Japan, the Americans accepted Chiang Kaishek and the GMD as the real force in China and therefore deserving of their full support. Yet it had not been out of the question for the Chinese Communists and the Americans to have reached an accommodation. Their interests in China often coincided, the most obvious example being their joint determination to defeat Japan. Moreover, at that stage their ideological differences were not an insurmountable hurdle. During the Japanese occupation, the CCP deliberately played down its political aims; it dropped its call for a class war and emphasised that it was engaged in a national struggle against the Japanese aggressor. Furthermore, the war in Europe which had witnessed a four-year military alliance between Communist USSR and capitalist USA was clear evidence that ideologies need not be a barrier to co-operation.

But such opportunities as the Japanese war offered for CCP-American detente were lost. In 1944 Mao put forward a plan for a CCP-GMD coalition government to run China once Japan had been defeated. Talks between the two parties were carried on for over a year, with Patrick Hurley, the American Ambassador being in frequent and supportive attendance. However, in March 1945 Chiang suddenly broke off the negotiations and declared that he had no intention of sharing power with the Communists. Hurley continued to back Chiang. But many of the US advisers and embassy officials were uneasy. In their reports to Washington they repeated the arguments advanced earlier by General Stilwell and his successor, General Wedemeyer, that Mao and his Communists represented a real social and political force in China; a GMD-CCP coalition was therefore both logical and desirable. It was a theme taken up by George Marshall, who was sent to China as President Truman's special envoy in December 1945. Marshall spent some months attempting to resurrect the GMD-CCP talks but by March 1946 he had to admit that Chiang's obduracy made a compromise settlement impossible.

Notwithstanding the advice of many of its experts on the spot, the USA formally maintained its policy of supporting Chiang Kaishek and the Nationalists. One reason for this apparent disregard of political realities was that by 1946 the USA had already committed huge resources to shoring up the GMD. Under a lend-lease scheme it had issued millions of dollars worth of military equipment to the Nationalists. It had provided transport to carry over half a million GMD troops to the zones surrendered by the Japanese, an operation described by Wedemeyer as 'the greatest air and sea transportation in history'. In addition, 55,000 US marines had been sent to the northern ports as 'military advisers' to the GMD. The USA judged that such an outlay made it impossible, particularly at a time of hardening Cold War stances, to make a major diversion in its Far Eastern policy. The result was that it continued to finance and support Chiang and the Nationalists, regardless of the fact that the GMD had long since forfeited the support of the majority of the Chinese people.

There is a notable revisionist argument that suggests that there was a brief 'pre-Cold War' period, between the Yalta Conference in February 1945 and the death of Roosevelt two months later, when Soviet-American co-operation was so amicable in regard to the imminent defeat of Germany that there was a real possibility it could be extended to an understanding over China. The argument runs that neither power at this point looked upon the other as necessarily a competitor in the Far East; there was no need, therefore, to take sides in the GMD-CCP dispute on ideological grounds. However, the succession of Harry S. Truman to the presidency on the death of Roosevelt meant that a conciliatory president was replaced by a hardliner with a natural distrust of the Soviet Union. By the time the Japanese war ended in August, the Soviet seizure of Manchuria on the one hand and the American occupation of northern Chinese ports on the other had created a mutual Soviet-American suspicion in the Far East that matched the cold war frigidities that were developing in Europe over the German and Berlin questions. Whatever credibility one gives to this argument, the reality was that from 1946 onwards Cold War divisions were replicated in the respective approaches of the USSR and the USA to the China question.

One of the USA's major mistakes was in viewing the Chinese Communists as simply an oriental form of Soviet Marxism. It failed to appreciate that the important emphasis in Chinese Communism was on the Chinese element. Mao and his followers had adopted Communism not primarily because of its political ideology, but because it provided a programme for a Chinese rejection of Western imperialism. Communism in China would always be modified by its proponents to make it fit the Chinese situation. Therefore, there was nothing inevitable about Sino-American hostility. For Mao, friendship with the USA would have been perfectly compatible with the pursuit of a Communist social programme in China. But the Americans judged Mao's Communism by the same standards they applied to the Soviet version. Again one has to emphasise the Cold War tensions that lay behind all this. The USA felt it had no choice; after 1945 it could not afford, in a starkly divided world, to take the risk of lessening its deep distrust of Communist objectives. Mao was dangerous because Communism was dangerous; an accommodation with him was diplomatically out of the question.

After 1949 the USA became greatly exercised over what it revealingly referred to as the 'loss of China'. American government officials and academics repeatedly asked themselves where they had gone wrong. Why, after so much investment in time, money and resources in China, had it fallen prey to Communism? Stalin and the USSR were seen as the obvious culprits. To the USA, China's 'going red' was part of a great world conspiracy engineered by the USSR. It appeared that following the victory of Mao's Communists in 1949, there stretched from East Germany eastwards to the Pacific one huge land mass that was subject to the ideology of Marxism and the leadership of Stalin. In the light of what is now known about the depth of Sino-Soviet animosity from the 1930s onwards, this mistaken judgement has a peculiar irony. But what governments do is determined by their current perceptions. The USA had simply lacked the necessary understanding of the Chinese situation to have acted otherwise.

```
┌─────────────────────────────────────────────┐
│              A study in ambivalence            │
└─────────────────────────────────────────────┘
┌─────────────────────────────────────────────────┐
│  China - the exploited  ◄──────► the West - the exploiter  │
├─────────────────────────────────────────────────┤
│   the West's economic / technological / military superiority │
│        challenges China's sense of uniqueness              │
├─────────────────────────────────────────────────┤
│   China's hatred of Western condescension and contempt      │
│                                                    │
│   China's need of Western captial and industrial know-how   │
└─────────────────────────────────────────────────┘
```

```
┌─────────────────────────────────────────────────┐
│        China's lack of international standing            │
│                                                    │
│  Chinese contribution to Allied cause in First World War │
│        China humiliated by the Versailles Treaty        │
│                                                    │
│ China a pawn in the postwar international realignment, 1920-31 │
└─────────────────────────────────────────────────┘
```

```
┌─────────────────────────────────────────────────┐
│   the West and the Sino-Japanese Conflict, 1931-41      │
├─────────────────────────────────────────────────┤
│              the absence of response                  │
│                                                    │
│  League of Nations - Britain - France - USSR - USA    │
└─────────────────────────────────────────────────┘
```

```
┌─────────────────────────────────────────────────┐
│     China and the Second World War, 1941-5           │
├─────────────────────────────────────────────────┤
│           China's elevation in status               │
│                                                    │
│           Chiang as world statesman                 │
├─────────────────────────────────────────────────┤
│     The USA and the 'loss' of China                 │
└─────────────────────────────────────────────────┘
```

Summary - China and the West

Studying *'China and the West'*

The chapter on China and the West can be conveniently broken down into five main sections: 1. China's subordination to the West; 2. China's economic relations with the West; 3. China's place in international relations; 4. China and the Second World War; 5. China's relations with the USA. Each of these themes raises questions which are central to an examination of the topic of China and the West.

1. China's subordination to the West

Key question: Why was the West in a position of dominance over China in the early twentieth century?

Sections 1 and 2 of this chapter are the obvious required reading but added perspective will be gained by consulting sections 1 to 3 of the Introduction and section 1 of Chapter 2.

Points to consider: Superior military technology had enabled the Western powers to impose themselves on the Chinese since the 1840s. By the end of the century, the major colonial powers had forced China to recognise their extra-territorial possessions and to grant them favoured commercial status. The defeat of China in the Sino-Japanese war in 1895 had encouraged further Western encroachments. In the 'scramble for concessions', France, Britain, Russia and Germany forced the Chinese to enter into a further series of 'unequal treaties'. China's difficulties were compounded by the strength of its neighbour, Japan, a strength that was evident in Japan's victory over Russia in 1905 and which was acknowledged in the Western powers' readiness to accord Japan equal diplomatic status with themselves.

While it is true that the USA warned the other imperial powers against treating China as another Africa to be carved up at their whim, America's apparent solicitude had less to do with a concern for China than a wish to exert its own influence over the western Pacific rim. There were sporadic Chinese protests against Western domination but these proved largely unsuccessful since they lacked leadership and co-ordination. This was manifest in the failure of the Manchus to turn the Boxer rising of 1900 into an effective national movement. Anxious to preserve their independence of central government, the local provincial and military leaders declined to co-operate with Beijing, preferring instead to align themselves with the international force in crushing the Boxers. The fact was that many Chinese were ambiguous in their attitude towards the West. Large numbers of them had come to depend economically and financially on the Western presence; they judged, therefore, that open resistance to the foreigner simply put their livelihoods at risk. Such inhibitions would not be overcome until China developed a political movement strong enough to convince the Chinese that they could achieve national regeneration and economic independence through their own efforts.

2. China's economic relations with the West

Key question: Distinguish between the economic advantages and disadvantages brought to China by its subordination to the West.

Section 3 of this chapter is the most relevant reading but it would also be helpful to refer to sections 1 to 3 of the Introduction.

Points to consider: Something of an industrial revolution occurred in China between 1890 and 1910. The incidence of low costs and high returns, guaranteed by the unequal treaties, made China an attractive market for Western investors and manufacturers. The situation was not so obviously advantageous for the Chinese. It was true, of course, that an inflow of foreign investment and the spread of Western-owned factories increased China's resources of capital and materiel. Yet China's economic weakness in relation to the West meant that it was chronically disadvantaged in its dealings with the international powers. Dependent on the foreign loans essential for its industrialisation programme, China was always in the position of a debtor. This was particularly evident in regard to the railways. The Manchu government borrowed heavily from abroad in order to create a national Chinese railway system. As a result, the Manchu dynasty left the Republic that succeeded it in 1912 a heavy burden of debt that could be met only by further borrowing. The continuation of Chinese indebtedness was a crippling limitation on China's aspirations towards genuine national independence.

But there were positive features to China's subjection to Western capitalism. Employment prospects for men and women and the chances of receiving regular and better wages were greatly improved for the Chinese by the expansion of Western industrial enterprises. Furthermore, the example of the success of Western companies stimulated the Chinese to develop their own businesses, which were quick to apply the lessons in management and structuring which they had learned. China was certainly exploited; the first thought of the international powers in China was to use the country for their own commercial and economic advantage. Yet without the contact with the West which it had to endure, it is unlikely that China would have generated the finance and resources or developed the economic understanding necessary for its own modernisation.

3. China's place in international relations

Key question: Why was it not until 1941 that the Western powers were prepared to support China in its struggle against Japan?

Sections 4, 5 and 6 of this chapter are the essential reading for this theme; reference should also be made to sections 4 to 6 of Chapter 6.

Points to consider: An appropriate starting point in assessing Western attitudes towards Sino-Japanese relations is the Washington Conference of 1921-2. Ostensibly, this gathering was called in order to draft guarantees of China's national sovereignty, but the real purpose of the major powers, France, Britain and the USA, was to check the growing strength of Japan in the Far East. The agreements produced during the Conference were concerned far more with the adjustment of relations between the powers than with China's rights. Although the Nine-Power

Agreement, signed at Washington, formally recognised Chinese independence, no practical steps were taken to end extra-territoriality or the unequal treaties. How little the West was prepared to protect Chinese integrity was clear from its failure to respond actively to Japan's increasing aggression towards China. The Japanese, convinced in the 1920s that the USA was seeking their ruin by imposing a trade block against them, compensated by seizing Chinese territory and resources. Japan justified its occupation of Manchuria in 1931 and its full-scale assault on China in 1937 as moves it had to make in order to avoid economic collapse. The Western powers, notwithstanding their commitment to the principle of collective security and their condemnation of Japan's actions, remained preoccupied with their own economic crises and made no military moves in the Far East. The League of Nations proved equally ineffective. Without an army and lacking the USA as a member, the League could pass resolutions but was incapable of action. The basic fact of international relations was that unless individual states felt their particular concerns to be involved they were not prepared to put themselves at risk for China. Indeed, commercial considerations led some Western companies to increase their trade with Japan between 1937 and 1941. It was for these reasons that in the early stages of the Sino-Japanese War, 1937-41, China stood alone. Not until December 1941, when the Japanese attack upon Pearl Harbor put the matter beyond all doubt, did the USA and the other Western powers feel themselves sufficiently threatened to declare war on Japan and thus come belatedly to the aid of China and then only as part of a greater war design.

4. China and the Second World War

Key question: Consider the view that the Second World War saved China but destroyed Chiang Kaishek

Sections 6, 7 and 8 of this chapter are the obvious required reading but it would also be helpful to consult sections 4 to 5 of Chapter 3.

Points to consider: It has been said that 8 December 1941 was the happiest day of Chiang Kaishek's life since it marked the entry of the USA into the Far Eastern struggle. The total war that America vowed to pursue transformed what had been a Chinese affair into a critical part of the much larger world conflict. As a vital ally, China would now receive very considerable American resources. In addition, China's enhanced status induced Britain and the USA in 1942 to abandon the unequal treaties and the principle of extra-territoriality. Such developments raised Chiang Kaishek to the rank of international statesman, the apparent confidant of Churchill and Roosevelt. At the Cairo Conference in 1943 Chiang was promised that, with the final defeat of Japan, China would recover all the territories and privileges it had lost since 1895.

But appearances were deceptive. The seeming respect paid to Chiang was expedient flattery designed to maintain his commitment to the Allied cause. China, moreover, was not invited to the Yalta Conference in 1945 at which the Americans made secret promises to Russia that it would receive the key areas, Mongolia and Manchuria, previously promised to China. Yet even this would not have mattered to Chiang had his basic dream been realised. For Chiang the importance of having America's support was that it made possible the fulfilment of his belief that in the course of defeating the Japanese the USA would also assist him in destroying his Communist enemies within. This is where the notion of betrayal, albeit an unwitting one, is particularly appropriate. The sudden way in which the atomic bombing of Japan brought the war to an end overturned all Chiang's calculations. The Japanese surrender made the anticipated large-scale American troop landings in China unnecessary. Chiang did not now have the American army to roll up the Communists. Although the USA continued to support Chiang during the ensuing GMD-CCP civil war from 1946-9 American assistance was not enough to stay the CCP's inexorable march to victory.

There is certainly a case for saying that such was the hold of the Japanese on China by 1941 that the Chinese could not have saved themselves by their own unaided efforts. It is equally arguable that the USA's entry into the war created in Chiang an understandable conviction that he now had at his disposal the means of obliterating his real enemies within China. The dramatic and unforeseen events of August 1945 were to destroy his hopes.

5. China's relations with the USA

Key question: In what sense had the USA 'lost' China by 1949?

The essential reading here is sections 7 and 8 of the current chapter. It would also be helpful to consult section 5 in the Introduction.

Points to consider: The term 'lost' suggests that in some sense the USA had previously held or possessed China. This is obviously an American perception relating to the USA's conviction that its diplomatic, military and financial investment in China before 1949 had created a special Sino-American relationship, which was destroyed by the Communist victory in 1949. In its eagerness to win the war against Japan, the USA accepted Chinese politics at face value and liaised with Chiang Kaishek, the acknowledged leader of China. In the subsequent four-year struggle the USA poured huge resources into China, in addition to granting Chiang and his GMD government full diplomatic recognition. In hindsight this may be seen as an error, in that the Americans gave insufficient attention to the internal situation in China, appearing to ignore the role Mao Zedong and the Communists were playing in leading Chinese resistance against Japan. Some of the USA's own Chinese experts warned the State Department that Chiang's strength was circumscribed and that power was shifting to Mao and the CCP.

However, even after the war with Japan had ended, the USA did not feel free to judge the Chinese situation on its own merits. The intrusion of Cold War politics after 1945 meant that the USA now read things ideologically. Unaware of the lack of affinity between the Soviet and Chinese brand of Communism, the USA felt unable to negotiate with Mao Zedong since it interpreted Chinese Communism as simply an oriental variant of Soviet Marxism. The USA, therefore, reaffirmed its commitment to Chiang Kaishek and continued to support the GMD even as it was being defeated and driven out of China by the CCP. The Americans 'lost' China by backing the wrong side. They did not grasp that Mao and his followers had adopted Communism primarily because of its anti-imperialism. Given the USA's own tradition of anti-colonialism, that might well have provided a common ground between East and West; in theory, an accommodation between Chinese Communism and American democracy was not impossible. Before 1949, Mao had frequently shown a willingness to negotiate with the Americans. But the USA before 1945 had been too preoccupied with the Japanese war, and after 1945 too conditioned by its Cold War with the USSR, to give balanced consideration to the forming of an understanding with Mao and the CCP. That is the context in which to define its loss of China.

Source analysis - *'China and the West'*

The following is an analysis of three related documents central to the theme of 'China and the West'. They appear on pages 71, 82 and 84.

1 - Context

All three extracts come from British sources. The first is from a leader of 1912 in *The Times* newspaper, a major voice of the British establishment, reflecting on the 1911 Chinese revolution. The second is part of the private comment by Winston Churchill, the British Prime Minister, on China's international standing in 1943. The third comes from the *Observer*, a 'quality' newspaper, regarded as representing progressive opinion in Britain, reflecting on the Sino-Soviet alliance of August 1945.

2 - Meaning

The Times expresses extreme doubt as to whether a deferential society like China, given the strength and longevity of its monarchical tradition, is capable of making the transition to a modern republic. Churchill's complaint thirty years later is that current talk of the war having raised China to world-power status comparable with Britain and the major nations of Europe is wildly unrealistic. The *Observer's* leader seeks to analyse the impact of the Sino-Soviet Treaty on the power balance between the CCP and the GMD in China. Believing that the CCP will receive no effective assistance from the USSR, the leader suggests that the Communists will be unable to mount a successful assault on the GMD government. It acknowledges that the CCP has won peasant support in northern China but argues that this is inadequate to offset the power that the GMD's control of China's commercial stongholds gives it. It accepts that were the Communists to seize large amounts of Japanese weaponry this might make them an irritant to Chiang's government, but asserts that without direct Soviet aid this situation would last only briefly. It concludes that the boost in morale given to the Nationalists by their victory over Japan, the success of their progressive policies, and the signing of the treaty with Russia has made them proof against the challenge of the CCP.

3 - Significance

The three sources combine to offer an instructive insight into the character of the British attitude at key moments in China's development in the first half of twentieth century. What unites the extracts is their common conviction that China's aspirations ran ahead of its competence to achieve them. *The Times,* a highly influential and representative organ, states unambiguously that China in 1912 is simply not ready for a republic. Its antique political system of national deference to a divine emperor cannot easily or swiftly be replaced by a modern, sophisticated Western structure. Churchill is even blunter, albeit in private, in pointing out the fallacy of assuming that backward China can be elevated to world-power status merely because it has become an important ally in wartime. It is significant that Churchill's public recognition of Chiang and China was not genuine; it had been given only at the USA's insistence.

The *Observer* is sympathetic to the GMD regime and does not consider the Chinese Communists capable of winning the civil war. Within four years, of course, the CCP's victory, showed that the *Observer* had seriously misread the situation. It might be noted that, in contrast, *The Times* had judged correctly about the incapacity of the 1912 Chinese Republic to survive while Churchill had seriously underestimated China's ability to develop into a world power. But the overall significance of the three sources is not whether their judgements or prophecies were right or wrong. What stands out is the scepticism with which British spokesmen looked upon China's efforts to modernise. In this, Britain was representative of the other Western imperial powers in China. The exploitative or patronising way in which the West had treated the Chinese since the 1840s had blunted rather than sharpened its understanding of China's true potential.

CHAPTER 5

China and Japan

1 Introduction: China, Japan and the West

In the middle years of the nineteenth century, Japan and China had shared a similar attitude to the outside world. Although traditionally hostile towards each other, these oriental neighbours had for centuries regarded themselves as superior cultures, looking upon other peoples as barbarians. Consequently, it came as a great shock to both nations when Western imperialism with its superior military and technological skills began to impose itself upon them from the 1840s onwards. Japan, like China, was forced to accept a series of 'unequal treaties' that opened its ports to European and U S shipping and obliged it to accept commercial terms that heavily favoured the foreign traders. These were startling revelations of how weak the oriental nations were in comparison to the West.

Japan's response, in marked contrast to China's, was swift, positive and successful. Determined that the way to combat the West was by emulating its most 'advanced' characteristics, the Japanese adopted a series of extensive reforms aimed at rapid modernisation along Western lines. This reassertion of national pride is particularly identified with the reign of the Emperor Meiji (1869-1914). Abandoning the age-old policy of Japanese exclusiveness, the Meiji regime initiated wide ranging economic and social changes. The Imperial Court used its power to centralise government and make its administration more efficient. Despite the authoritarian nature of the regime, a written constitution was introduced, a move intended to impress the outside world.

Important economic advances were also occurring. Japan's rapidly multiplying population spread from the land to swell the cities and urban areas, thereby providing a huge labour resource. Industrial growth was seen as the basis of genuine modernisation and was given priority in state planning. Methods of taxation and revenue raising were modified to serve industrial needs. Between 1870 and 1914, output in such areas as mining, textiles and engineering, rose impressively. These economic developments were accompanied by major social and legal adjustments. A new civil code and a compulsory system of education, both built on European models, were introduced. Not surprisingly, such major alterations in Japanese society caused considerable unrest, but the Meiji regime was quick to crush any incipient signs of protest. The enforced social changes were backed by the use of powerful military force. Nor were the armed services simply a means of suppressing opposition. Militarism became a potent expression of Japan's new self-belief. By the turn of the century the Japanese army, structured on the German system, and the navy, modelled on the British, had developed a fearsome military capability. This was dramatically evident in Japan's crushing defeat of China in 1895 and of Russia in 1905. Triumph in war united the Japanese nation, sanctified the concept of martial glory, and attracted foreign investment.

A remarkable feature of Japan's emergence as a modern state was its success in reconciling cultural and religious traditions with the demands of modernity in such a way as to create a profound sense of national identity. Recognition by the rest of the world of Japan's equal status in international affairs became a basic Japanese ambition. This had an important cultural dimension. Japan took great pains to develop the high arts; galleries, museums and concert halls proliferated. In 1888 the London *Times* observed 'Tokyo has become the capital of the artistic world'. Japan's economic and cultural renaissance put it in a position internationally from which it successfully renegotiated the 'unequal treaties'. By the end of the century, Japan had achieved a parity with the West which enabled it to turn to thoughts of imperial expansion. The 1895 victory over China, the old enemy, was rewarded with large accessions of territory, including Korea and Taiwan. Between 1895 and 1900 Japan joined the European powers in 'the battle of the concessions', establishing extra-territorial enclaves in the major Chinese cities. Japanese forces were also involved in putting down the Boxer Risings in 1900. Chinese humiliation at the hands of her neighbour could hardly have been greater.

Japan's triumph in the Russo-Japanese War of 1904-5 was a remarkable proof of how far it had advanced in the world. The war had been preceded by a great diplomatic coup, the Anglo-Japanese Alliance of 1902, in which the two powers acknowledged each other's special interests in China and agreed to remain neutral in the event of the other's going to war with a third party. This gave Japan a free hand in its conflict with Russia two years later. The war was followed by the Russo-Japanese peace settlement of 1905, which in effect recognised the supremacy of Japan in east Asia.

At every major point of comparison with Japan, political, economic, military and diplomatic, China had been found wanting. Indeed, in many respects Japan's rise had been directly at the expense of China. China's resentment at foreign occupation was as intense as Japan's but it lacked the administrative and military organisation to mount an effective resistance. Geographically, the sheer size of China made it difficult to achieve the unity of purpose reached by her smaller, tightly knit, neighbour. Thus it was that Japan and China entered the twentieth century; Japan was united, prosperous, assertive, and able to claim equality with the West, whereas China was fragmented, bankrupt, subservient, and at the mercy of the West. This meant that their old rivalry would continue into the twentieth century in the form of Japan's persistent efforts to use her strength to exploit China's weakness. As a Japanese cabinet minister put it: 'We shall pluck the fruit off the withered tree'. One of the first fruits to be so plucked was

Korea, which Japan formally annexed in 1910.

It should be recorded that not all Japanese were happy with China's humiliation. A small but significant minority believed that the genuine liberation of Asia from foreign control required that Japan and China should act together in a common anti-Western policy. As a practical expression of that belief, 600 Japanese students went to China in 1911-12 to join the revolution. However, the collapse of the Manchus made little immediate difference to China's subordination to Japan. The rivalry between Yuan Shikai and Sun Yatsen in the early years of the Republic prevented any positive steps being taken to regenerate China. The notion of mutual Sino-Japanese interests did not entirely disappear but the prevailing view of the Tokyo government was that the chronic weakness of China called for a policy of exploitation not co-operation.

2 The Impact of the First World War on Sino-Japanese Relations

The outbreak of the European war in 1914 provided Japan with further opportunity to assert itself over China. Both countries had good reasons for offering to help the Allies; each hoped to gain the territories which Germany held in the Far East. In response to Britain's appeal for naval assistance, Japan actively supported the Allies from August 1914 onwards. China, however, did not enter the war until 1917. This gave Japan an obvious precedence over China in the eyes of the Allies. The struggle in Europe also gave Japan a freer hand to interfere in China while the Western powers were preoccupied with their own war effort. In 1915 the Japanese government presented Yuan Shikai with the '21 Demands', a peremptory set of requirements that, if accepted, would have destroyed China's independence. The Western Allies, Britain in particular, objected only to those demands which would have given Japan too great a freedom in maritime matters. Japan shrewdly withdrew these, but insisted that China accept the remainder. The following extracts indicate the character of the demands:

1 The Chinese Government engages to give full assent to all matters upon which the Japanese Government may hereafter agree with the German Government relating to the disposition of all rights, interests, and concessions which ... Germany possesses in relation
5 to the Province of Shantung ...
    Japanese subjects shall be free to reside and travel in South Manchuria and Eastern Inner Mongolia and to engage in business and in manufacture of any kind whatsoever ... The Chinese Government agrees that if it employs political, financial, or military
10 advisers or instructors in South Manchuria or Eastern Inner Mongolia, the Japanese Government shall first be consulted ...

Without the previous consent of Japan, China shall not by her
own act dispose of the rights and property of whatsoever nature of
[specified commercial] companies nor cause the said companies to
15 dispose freely of the same ...
    The Chinese Central Government shall employ influential
Japanese as advisers in political, financial, and military affairs ...
The police departments of the important places (in China) shall be
jointly administered by Japanese and Chinese [and] the police
20 departments of these places shall employ numerous Japanese ...
China shall purchase from Japan a fixed amount of munitions of
war (say 50 percent or more of what is needed by the Chinese)
    If China needs foreign capital to work mines, build railways, and
construct harbour-works (including dock-yards) in the Province of
25 Fukien, Japan shall be first consulted ...
    China agrees that Japanese subjects shall have the right to
propagate Buddhism in China.

Yuan, who was seeking to make himself acceptable to the Japanese, gave
in to these demands. His surrender created a violent outburst of anger
among the Chinese. Demonstrations and strikes occurred widely in
Beijing and other provincial cities. Significantly, the resentment was
directed as much against the new republican government as against
Japan. All the main sections of the Chinese community currently
dissatisfied with the Republic - students, traders, lawyers, teachers and
even some local officials - came together in open and spontaneous
defiance. For the first time the Chinese had shown a degree of popular
resistance strong enough to threaten officialdom. Yuan's capitulation to
the Japanese had further weakened his position as president. When, in
1916, he sought to turn his authority into that of emperor by
re-instituting the imperial throne with himself upon it, the gesture
proved a futile one. In China's straitened circumstances, Yuan's claim
to have inherited the imperial dignity appeared absurd. At the time of his
death a few months later, such power as he had held had already drained
away.
    Yuan's passing did little to clarify the situation. The semblance of
central authority that the Republic had exercised broke down and China
returned to being a collection of regions rather than a nation. Japan's
dominance thus increased and was further enhanced by the developments in the European war. In the final stages of that struggle, the Allies,
under President Woodrow Wilson's prompting, adopted self-determination as the principle upon which postwar international reconstruc-
tion would be based. This principle, if honoured, would both invalidate
Germany's right to possess colonies in the Far East and sanction their
reclamation by the Asian nations who had originally owned them. When
the Chinese formally entered the war on the Allied side in July 1917 they
did so in the expectation that they would be a major beneficiary in any

peace settlement. Unfortunately for them, Japan's claim to those same possessions was equally confidently held.

In separate and contradictory promises, the Allies had led both China and Japan to believe that each would be given the territory it claimed. Since it was the same territory in question, the commitment must necessarily betray one of the claimants. Given the imbalance of power between Japanese and the Chinese, there could be only one outcome - Japan would gain at China's expense. In April 1919 it was duly announced at the Paris Peace Conference that Japan was to be rewarded with Shandong, the province which China had expected to recover. The protests of the Chinese delegates at Versailles were pointedly ignored. As had happened in 1915, this humiliation gave rise to violent anti-Japanese demonstrations from those sections of the Chinese civilian population which regarded their government as craven and irresponsible. The sense of betrayal stimulated a range of political reactions, which became known collectively as the 4 May Movement. However, at this stage Chinese resistance was not sufficiently organised or centralised to be able to provide an effective challenge to the Japanese presence.

3 Japanese Designs on China

An interested observer of events in the Far East was the USA. In 1919 the US Congress had declined to support Woodrow Wilson's initiative in creating a League of Nations and had returned to an isolationist foreign policy. As a further step towards disengagement, the USA hosted the Washington Naval Conference in 1922. At this gathering, the major maritime nations, including Japan, signed a Nine-Power Agreement in which they undertook to recognise each other's respective spheres of influence. This apparently gave America confidence that its interests in the Pacific would not now be subject to Japanese threat. Had this been followed by the USA's offering trade terms to Japan, that indeed might have been the outcome. But rather than encourage commerce, the USA did the reverse; it adopted a high tariff policy which severely restricted its import of foreign goods. The result was that at a critical moment in its economic history Japan was deprived of an essential trade outlet. Without access to the American market, the Japanese could not make the profits necessary for the purchase of their essential raw materials. The consequent economic recession in Japan encouraged those elements in the government which argued that only by an aggressive expansionist policy could the nation gain the territories and resources that it required to sustain its growth. This, in turn, strengthened the case for further encroachment on Chinese territory as a step towards a much wider Japanese control of east Asia and the western Pacific. Such plans were the forerunners of what became known as the 'Greater East Asian Co-Prosperity Sphere', a Japanese euphemism for its own imperial expansion.

So, despite having promised in the Nine-Power Agreement to respect Chinese sovereignty and to return the disputed territory of Shandong, Japan made little effort to hide its intentions towards China. This intensified the anti-foreigner bitterness among the Chinese. In 1925 there occurred the 30 May Incident, a violent demonstration against the Japanese presence in China, which in its passion matched the 4 May Movement of six years earlier. However, with China still lacking a strong central government, weakened by the warlords, and divided by the hostility between the GMD and the Communists, only token resistance to the Japanese could be mounted at this stage.

a) The Tanaka Memorial, 1927

The disorder created by the 30 May Incident was eagerly seized upon by the Japanese as a justification for tightening their hold on China. The war party in the imperial cabinet, which was becoming an increasingly dominant influence in Japanese foreign policy, demanded the occupation of Manchuria and Mongolia as the first step in Japan's conquest of the whole of Asia. Their view was powerfully expressed in the Tanaka Memorial, a document that took its name from the petition submitted to the Emperor in 1927 by General Tanaka, the Prime Minister. The Memorial urged that Japan should abandon the promise it had given in 1922 at the Washington Naval Conference to honour Chinese sovereignty. The argument was that Japan's demographic and economic needs made it imperative that Manchuria be occupied; as well as being a source of urgently required raw materials the region was also needed as living space for the empire's expanding population.

1 The territory [Manchuria and Mongolia] is more than three times
  as large as our own empire, but it is inhabited by only one-third as
  many people. The attractiveness of the land does not arise from the
  scarcity of population alone; its wealth of forestry, minerals and
5 agricultural products is also unrivalled elsewhere in the world ...
    The restrictions of the Nine-Power Treaty have reduced our
  special rights and privileges in Manchuria and Mongolia to such an
  extent that there is no freedom left for us. The very existence of our
  country is endangered. Unless these obstacles are removed, our
10 national existence will be insecure ...
    In Japan her food supply and raw materials decrease in
  proportion to her population. If we merely hope to develop trade,
  we shall eventually be defeated by England and America, who
  possess unsurpassable capitalistic power. In the end we shall get
15 nothing. A more dangerous factor is the fact that the people of
  China might some day wake up. Even during these years of

internal strife, they can still toil patiently, and try to imitate and
displace our goods so as to impair the development of our trade.
When we remember that the Chinese are our sole customers, we
20 must beware lest one day China becomes unified and her
industries become prosperous. Americans and Europeans will
compete with us; our trade in China will be wrecked ...
  The way to gain actual rights in Manchuria and Mongolia is to
use this region as a base and, under the pretence of trade and
25 commerce, penetrate the rest of China. Armed by the rights
already secured we shall seize the resources all over the country.
Having China's entire resources at our disposal we shall proceed to
conquer India, the Archipelago, Asia Minor, Central Asia, and
even Europe. But to get control of Manchuria and Mongolia is the
30 first step. Final success belongs to the country having raw
materials; the full growth of national strength belongs to the
country having extensive territory. If we pursue a positive policy to
enlarge our rights in Manchuria and China, all these prerequisites
of a powerful nation will constitute no problem. Furthermore, our
35 surplus population of 700,000 each year will also be taken care of.

It is necessary for historical balance not to see Japan's hostility towards
China simply as naked aggression. There was in Japan at this time a real
sense of crisis, a profound fear that unless it took immediate steps to
acquire living space for its population and resources for its industries it
would be unable to sustain itself as a modern state. Those Japanese
whose attitude was represented by the Tanaka Memorial were
convinced that China's vast land mass, Britain's worldwide imperial
possessions, and the USA's gigantic industrial power, gave each of those
nations advantages denied to Japan. Thus the foreign policy followed by
the Japanese between the two world wars was driven by a conviction that
time was against them; if they did not seize the moment to expand their
territory and resources Japan would enter a period of irreversible
national decline.
  From time to time doubts have been cast on the authenticity of the
Tanaka Memorial. There have been suggestions that it was a Chinese
forgery drawn up with the obvious intention of causing acute diplomatic
embarrassment to the Japanese. But the charge of fabrication remains
unproved. What is even more important is that the document was an
exact formulation of Japan's prevailing attitude and intention towards
China. In all essentials Japanese policy from 1927 onwards was
conducted in conformity to the programme and spirit of the Memorial.
Moreover, the Memorial's analysis of Japan's economic position was
undeniably realistic. China was essential to Japan's well being. Over 80
per cent of Japan's total overseas investments were in China and the
greater part of those were in Manchuria. China accounted for a quarter
of Japan's international trade, with Manchuria as the principal

import-export region. There was thus an economic exigence behind the Japanese demand that Manchuria was too important to Japan's economic survival to be left independent. Of course, it was hardly to be expected that the Chinese, who were the major victims of their neighbour's thrust for modernity, would understand, let alone accept, the remorseless logic that underlay Japanese expansion. Nonetheless, it is important for the historian to appreciate the anxieties that motivated Japan's foreign policy and not to dismiss it merely as irrational oriental militarism.

It should also be emphasised that politically Japan was far from being totally united at this time. Factions within the country argued over the correct character and pace of the nation's development. This political divide was matched by disagreements between the two main wings of Japan's armed forces. The predominant view of the army was that the greatest danger to the nation came from the USSR which wanted to exploit China as a base from which to overwhelm Japan. Army analysts claimed that Russia, still smarting from its defeat at Japanese hands in 1905, was intent on regaining the former tsarist territories in the Far East. In contrast, the Japanese admiralty held strongly that the greater threat was not the USSR but the USA, whose naval strength in the Pacific was a barrier to legitimate Japanese expansion; therefore, Japan's pressing need was to develop a strategy that encompassed the waging of a successful naval war against America.

As the outbreak of war with the USA in 1941 was to show, it was the Japanese navy's perception that eventually prevailed. However, in the 1920s and 1930s, it was the army's viewpoint that predominated. The generals and their civilian spokesmen deliberately fostered an atmosphere of tension and crisis, claiming that unless Japan immediately protected its Chinese flank it would be open to Soviet incursion. What gave strength to the war party's argument was the contraction in international trade that accompanied the worldwide economic depression in the 1930s. Japan could no longer sell her goods abroad. This commercial crisis made it imperative that Japan consolidate its hold over Asia as a means of avoiding economic ruin.

4 The Japanese Occupation of Manchuria, 1931-7

The Japanese were cynical in their dealings with China. They secretly sought to destabilise the Chinese Republic while at the same time openly claiming that the weakness of China gave them a right to interfere there in order to protect Japan's vital interests. It is true that there was disagreement among the Japanese leaders over this two-faced approach. There were voices calling for restraint, but these tended to be shouted down by the hawks in the cabinet. This was evident in the Mukden Incident, the event that provided the pretext for the Japanese invasion of Manchuria in 1931. In what is still a cloudy affair, it appears that a group of Japanese officers in the Kwantung army, stationed in Manchuria, concocted a plot in which they blew up a stretch of the southern Manchurian railway at Mukden and then blamed the act on Chinese saboteurs. The officers, who were in league with the war party in Tokyo, then appealed to the Japanese government to authorise the punishment of the Chinese rebels. Without waiting for a response, the Kwantung army launched a full-scale sweep across Manchuria. Within six months the province was under Japanese military occupation. The Tokyo government, which had been initially reluctant to give unqualified backing to the Kwantung army, found itself swept along by war mania in Japan. Against the judgement of its more moderate members, the government sanctioned the takeover of Manchuria and then defended its actions against the international protests that followed. The League of Nations, to whom Chiang Kaishek appealed, passed resolutions condemning the Japanese action but was powerless to alter the situation. In any case, Japan showed its contempt for international opinion by wholly ignoring the resolutions and then formally withdrawing from the League in 1933.

In 1932 the Japanese consolidated their occupation of Manchuria by formally changing its name to Manchukuo and declaring it to be an independent Chinese nation, ruled by Pu Yi, the last emperor of the Qing dynasty. But in reality it was a puppet state with a puppet leader under direct Japanese control. As with the Mukden Incident, the creation of Manchukuo was the result of a local Japanese initiative which the Tokyo government was then pressured into accepting. The aggressive-expansionist drive in Japan was gaining an unstoppable momentum.

Japan's seizure of Manchuria in 1931 proved to be the first stage in a Sino-Japanese conflict that was to last until 1945. It was a struggle that fundamentally changed the course of Chinese history. The internal political conflict within China was to be determined by the way the war was conducted and eventually concluded. The initial reaction of the Chinese parties to the occupation of Manchuria was to unite against Japan as the common enemy. But from the beginning, the unity was more apparent than real. Chiang Kaishek always regarded resistance to Japan as secondary to his aim of destroying the Communists. His basic strategy was to give ground before the Japanese invaders, judging that they would never be able to conquer such a vast country as China. Although there were occasions when he found it expedient to unite with the Reds against the invader, his priority remained the crushing of the Communist enemy within China.

In any case, whatever the United Front's declared objectives may have been, there was little chance of realising them immediately; Japan was too powerfully entrenched. The approach of the Japanese to their occupation of China had two main features. At the same time as they increased their control over the Chinese, their ministers endeavoured to create harmonious relations with China's leaders. This apparent contradiction followed from Japan's readiness, when expedient, to emphasise the racial and historical links that bound the two peoples together. Japan argued that it made perfect sense to look towards a common Sino-Japanese future. Having been rebuffed by the Americans, the Japanese were anxious to make east Asia an area of oriental resistance to Western cultural and economic hegemony. In 1936, Hirota Koki, Japan's Foreign Minister, showed intense irritation at the GMD's attempt to negotiate a special loan from the USA. Koki complained that Japan was now sufficient for all China's needs and quoted the mutuality of their interests. Yet he punctuated his appeal to the common links between the two nations with demands that the Chinese recognise Japan's special rights and privileges in China. Clearly, Japanese notions of co-operation rested on the assumption that Japan would remain very much the dominant partner. This was evident in Japan's insistence on the creation of the East Hubei Autonomous Council, which in theory was a new independent Chinese government, but was in fact simply a front behind which the Japanese maintained their control.

5 China and Japan at War, 1937-45

The Sino-Japanese war divides into two distinct sections: 1937-41 and 1941-5. During the first phase Japan made rapid advances down the eastern seaboard (see the map on page 106) to which the Chinese response was a mixture of unavailing resistance and appeasement. The second phase saw the Chinese struggle subsumed into the Second World War with the USA as China's main ally.

a) 1937-41

The United Front of Communists and Nationalists, which was reformed after the Xian Incident in 1936, brought together the two former antagonists, thus suggesting that China could unite in resistance to the invader. However, this apparently successful co-operation was marred by Chiang's grudging conformity to the Xian agreement. For him the real enemy remained the Communists, and where possible he diverted forces and materials to their destruction rather than to that of the Japanese. As a result, breaches of the United Front were constant, most of them perpetrated by the GMD.

Whatever the real strength of the United Front, the Japanese determined to act quickly to deny it the chance to give backbone to Chinese resistance. On 7 July 1937 (the 'Double Seventh'), a relatively minor clash between Chinese and Japanese troops at the Marco Polo Bridge, ten miles outside Beijing, became the pretext for Japan to demand still more concessions from the GMD government. On this

occasion, Chiang Kaishek refused. He declared to the Chinese people
that their country was now in a state of total war against Japan: 'If we
allow one inch more of our territory to be lost, we shall be guilty of an
unpardonable crime against our race'. This was very much in the spirit
of the Xian agreement. It seemed to betoken a new commitment on
Chiang's part to lead the United Front in genuine resistance to
occupation. But his resolve was to wax and wane; throughout the
ensuing eight years of the Sino-Japanese war, Chiang's principal aim
remained the defeat of the Communists; victory over Japan was a means
to that end.

Nonetheless, there was little doubt that his stand in 1937 was a
powerful symbol of China's will to fight. From that date on, until 1945,
a bitter Sino-Japanese struggle ensued. Initially, matters went badly for
the Chinese. By 1938, Beijing, Shanghai, Ghangzhou and Nanjing had
all fallen to Japan, disasters which obliged the GMD government to
withdraw their capital to Chongqing (see the map on page 106). The
savagery of the Japanese excesses after the fall of Nanjing appalled
international opinion. The following is an extract from the evidence at
the war-crimes tribunal held by the Allies in 1947:

1 Because of the fact that the defenders of Nanjing had continued to
   resist and refused to surrender, the Japanese army, after capturing

The aftermath of a Japanese air raid on Shanghai, 1937

the city, conducted a systematic campaign of murder to show its revenge, hatred, and frustration ...

5   The total number of civilians and prisoners of war who fell victim to this campaign of mass murder was well beyond 300,000. Dead bodies were piled from one street corner to another, and no words, however eloquent, were adequate enough to describe this atrocity of unprecedented scale.

10   For instance, at 1 p.m. of December the fifteenth [1937], 2,000 of the city's police force, having been captured by the Japanese army, were marched toward an area outside of the Hanchung Gate where they were systematically machine-gunned. Those who were wounded were subsequently buried alive ...

15   On December 14, Yao Chia-lung was ordered to watch the performance when Japanese soldiers took turns raping his wife. When his eight-year-old son and three-year-old daughter pleaded for mercy on behalf of their mother, the rapers picked them up with their bayonets and roasted them to death over a camp fire. From 20 December 13 to 17 a large number of Japanese troops took turns raping a young maiden in the street outside of the Chunghua Gate; and, when a group of Buddhist monks passed by, they were ordered to rape this girl too. After the monks had refused to comply with this order, the Japanese cut off their penises, an act 25 which caused the monks to bleed to death .... Because of this widespread raping, no woman in the city felt safe and a large number of these frightened women took refuge in the specifically designated 'safety zone' operated by the International Commission. But the Japanese paid no heed to international law or justice. 30 At night they climbed the wall that surrounded the 'safety zone' and descended upon the women inside. They raped all and any who happened to be nearby, regardless of age and other considerations. Wherever the Japanese army went, they burned as well as committed mass murder. Since Nanjing, being our capital, 35 was designated as the primary area to practise terror, it was among the most thoroughly burned of the Chinese cities. After the city fell, almost one half of the city was reduced to ashes.

Although the behaviour of the troops in this instance was not officially sanctioned by Tokyo, the Japanese army in China had soon gained a worldwide notoriety for the brutal way it treated both its military and civilian captives. Attempts have been made to explain this as an aspect of Japan's bushido (warrior) cult, and more specifically as an act of retribution for a massacre of Japanese personnel by Chinese troops at Tungchow in July 1937. But it is significant that the Japanese government was at pains to prevent its own people from learning of the gratuitous violence that invariably accompanied Japan's military conquests.

As Japan gained ground in China it endeavoured to consolidate its

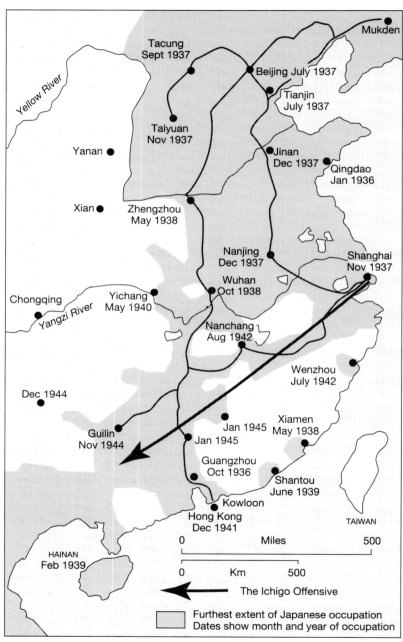

The Sino-Japanese War 1937-45

military hold by enlisting Chinese leaders who were willing to co-operate in the setting up of nominally independent areas. The official Japanese line was that they were aiming to create a new economic order, 'the East Asia Co-Prosperity Sphere', based on the harmonious working together of Japan and China. The Japanese identified Communism as the major enemy. In an effort to weaken the United Front, Tokyo offered to recognise Chiang Kaishek as the national spokesman for China if he would abandon his alliance with the CCP. The alternative, he was told, was a continuation and expansion of the Japanese occupation. Chiang refused. While it is true that Chiang's ultimate objective was the defeat of the Reds, he was never willing to compromise his claim to the leadership of China by throwing in his lot with the Japanese.

However, there were lesser public figures who were prepared to respond to the Japanese approaches. One such was Wang Jingwei, a former GMD colleague of Chiang. Motivated by a mixture of personal ambition and a real conviction that China could not win the war against Japan, Wang agreed in 1940 to become the head of what the Japanese called 'the New Government of China'. From Nanjing, the captured former capital, Wang denounced Chiang Kaishek and his Nationalist Government at Chongqing as traitors to the true interests of China and no longer deserving of the support of the people. Wang Jingwei's rival government survived for four years until Wang's death in 1944. It was not a total charade. It was recognised by the Axis powers, and many of the ordinary Chinese who lived within its jurisdiction had reason to be thankful for its ability to obtain more humane treatment for them from the Japanese. But the 'New Government' was never able to match either the GMD at Chongqing or the Reds at Yanan as expressions of Chinese aspirations. Without the backing of the occupying forces, Wang's government, as with the other 'autonomous' regional administrations established by the Japanese, would have been powerless.

International tensions and preoccupations meant that Japan's full-scale attack upon the Chinese mainland between 1937 and 1941 met no significant foreign opposition. Consequently, Japan was able to overrun large parts of the central and southern coastline of China, and make major incursions inland. By 1940 Japan had committed over three-quarters of a million ground troops to the struggle. This was a huge drain on men and materiel. But once Japan had made the commitment, it could not easily detach itself unless it achieved complete victory. Down to 1941 this outcome seemed highly probable, but that year marked the great turning point in the Sino-Japanese struggle. Ironically this momentous change, which led ultimately to the destruction of Japan, was of Japan's own making. On 7 December 1941 Japanese airforces launched 'Operation Tora Tora', an unannounced attack upon the US Pacific fleet, moored at Pearl Harbor in Hawaii. Japan claimed to have been provoked into this action by the USA's attempt earlier in 1941 to impose a total international embargo on oil supplies to Japan, a ban that had been intended to destroy the Japanese economy.

b) 1941-5

With hindsight, it is evident that Japan's attack on the USA was a fatal move. In a prolonged war, Japan stood no chance of defeating the USA, the world's most powerful economic and military state. But at the time, Japanese thinking ran along the following lines. A quick, disabling, strike on the US Pacific forces would oblige the American government to make an immediate peace on Japanese terms. Japan had no territorial designs on the American mainland; its essential aim was to drive America out of the Pacific, leaving Japan free to reach its natural extension as an Asiatic power. The gamble failed because the Japanese had not allowed for the depth of outrage with which America reacted to the attack. President Roosevelt's bitter condemnation of 'this day of infamy' expressed the passionate conviction with which the Americans entered what they characterised as a crusade against Japanese barbarism. In declaring war, the USA resolved upon the total defeat of Japan. Although for another eighteen months after Pearl Harbor, Japan, driven by the need to increase its oil supplies, continued to extend itself as far south as the Philippines and as far west as Burma, this very expansion meant that it had overstretched itself. Should the war prove a protracted one, the strain upon Japanese resources would become unbearable. It is true that Japan fought for four years, 1941-5, with extraordinary fervour but, even before the atomic bombing of the Japanese mainland in August 1945 brought its resistance to an end, it was already clear that Japan would not achieve its original objectives.

The importance for China of Japan's attack on the USA in 1941 was profound. What had been an essentially Sino-Japanese conflict now became a vital theatre of the much larger world war. From that time on, China was seen by the Allies as a chief means of defeating Japan. It was supplied with vast resources in an Allied effort to turn it into a base of operations. By 1945 the USA had invested over one billion dollars in China. Moreover, America's entry gave a tremendous boost to Chiang Kaishek as Chinese leader. It is said that Chiang declared 8 December 1941 to be the happiest day of his life. It is easy to see why. The Americans, anxious to use China principally as a means of defeating Japan, turned naturally to Chiang. As the leader of China, acknowledged as such even by the CCP under the Xian agreement, he was the obvious person with whom to liaise. All Chiang's public pronouncements were intended to convince the Allies that he was not merely to be trusted but that he was indeed the only real hope of a successful unifying of the Chinese war effort against Japan. President Roosevelt came to regard Chiang Kaishek as being as important a world figure in wartime as Churchill or Stalin.

Yet, despite the influx after 1941 of American money and supplies, Chiang and the GMD remained reluctant to face the Japanese head on. There were few pitched battles between Chinese and Japanese forces. To avoid being overwhelmed by the superior Japanese armies, the Chinese necessarily fought a guerilla war. This did not prevent the cities and urban areas suffering severely from Japanese air strikes. It was in the GMD-held areas in the south that the Japanese found the easiest targets to bomb. Chongqing, for example, suffered intermittent periods of aerial bombardment, similar in their destruction and terror to the blitz experienced in British and German cities between 1940 and 1945. Nonetheless, for most of the war, it was the Reds at their base in Yanan, not the Nationalists at Chongqing, who bore the brunt of the fighting.

Chiang Kaishek proved a difficult ally after 1941. He frequently quarrelled with the American advisers and demanded that those he disagreed with be replaced. Anxious not to weaken the war effort, the USA tended to do as he asked, despite the charge made by many American observers that Chiang's perverse preoccupation with crushing the Reds was a principal cause of China's poor showing against the Japanese. This was the essential complaint of General Stilwell, one of Chiang's sharpest critics. Stilwell observed that, compared to the CCP's struggle against Japan, the GMD's resistance was half-hearted and ineffective; invaluable American resources were being wasted on the Nationalists. Anxious to avoid antagonising Chiang, the State Department replaced Stilwell, but substance was given to his argument by the outcome of the Ichigo offensive of 1944, the largest campaign undertaken in China by the Japanese. The GMD armies were unable to stem the advance which carried Japanese forces deep into southern China. It was not merely that the GMD was worsted in military terms; it was evident that their armies lacked the will to fight. Chiang's critics did not find this surprising. The GMD's savage methods of recruitment and ferocious discipline were hardly calculated to inspire loyalty and enthusiasm among their troops. Reasonably competent when things were going well, the Nationalist forces too often broke when put under pressure. Their problems were compounded by their failure to win the whole-hearted support of the Chinese people whose protector they supposedly were. Indeed, an outstanding feature of the war was the unpopularity of the GMD armies among the Chinese peasantry. This was a product of the abusive treatment the peasants invariably received at the hands of the Nationalist troops and of the GMD government's harsh taxation and expropriation policies.

What eventually saved the GMD forces from total rout was not the quality of their resistance but the curtailing of Japan's war effort in China as the Japanese mainland fell under increasing Allied attack from 1944 onwards. The climax of the aerial onslaught came with the atomic bombing of Japan by the USA in August 1945. Within a few days of the unleashing of this awesome new power against them, the Japanese surrendered. The abrupt end of the Pacific war dramatically changed the position in China. From 1941 onwards, Chiang had calculated that American support would hand him eventual victory over both Japan and the CCP. He was to be disappointed. The use of the atom bomb against Japan in 1945 brought a sudden end to the war, leaving the Communists unconquered. The Japanese war, which earlier had held for Chiang the promise of success over all his rivals, had in the end exposed his weakness.

This became apparent at the end of the war in relation to the dispute over the Japanese surrender. The Communists naturally assumed the right to receive the formal submission of the Japanese forces in the nineteen liberated areas of northern China. Zhu De and Mao Zedong ordered their troops to occupy the former Japanese-held regions and hold the Japanese prisoners. Chiang's government at Chongqing, however, insisted that the Japanese should surrender only to accredited representatives of the GMD. But the problem for the GMD was that they could not enforce this demand; they had no troops in the Communist-dominated areas. Chiang, therefore, instructed the Japanese to continue to maintain order and discipline in their areas until GMD forces arrived. The same orders were sent to the 'autonomous regions' which the Japanese had formerly set up. The Nationalists would have been unable to succeed in this had the USA not stepped in. Anxious to prevent the Soviet Union, whose forces were already in Manchuria, from extending its control southwards, the Americans mounted a huge airlift of GMD forces to the liberated areas. General MacArthur, the Allied Commander-in-Chief in the Far East, declared that only Chiang Kaishek had the right to receive Japan's surrender in China. The question now was whether the Communists would accept this. Although Mao condemned Chiang and the GMD as 'fascists', he announced that he was willing to make the necessary concession. Mao explained why to his followers:

> Without theses concessions, we will not be able to shatter the GMD's plot for civil war, nor take the political initiative, nor gain the sympathy of the rest of the world ... nor gain legal status for our party.

Angered though he was by the American initiative, Mao knew that the recent Soviet-GMD friendship treaty meant that he was unlikely to receive support from the USSR should he openly challenge Chiang's American-backed claims over the surrender issue. Despite Mao Zedong's caution at this stage, it would soon become clear that the net result of the Sino-Japanese war had been to leave the Communists in a position of strength in China from which, within five years, they were able to take control of the whole of China. The Japanese war had served as the great catalyst in Chinese politics.

Western Colonialism Impacted on the Far East
|
the response

Japan	China
positive	negative
|	|
the Meiji reforms	antiquated system remains
|	|
economic modernisation	static economy
|	|
military strength	military weakness

Japan and China enter the twentieth century

Japan	China
|	|
united, prosperous, assertive on a par with the West	fragmented, bankrupt, subservient at the mercy of the West

The Assertion of Japanese Superiority
the 21 Demands, 1915
Japan rewarded with Shandong and Qingdao
the Tanaka Memorial, 1927
the occupation of Manchuria, 1931
the East Asian Co-Prosperity Sphere concept
China invaded and occupied, 1937-45
the Second World War, 1941-5
the saviour of China

Summary - China and Japan

Studying 'China and Japan'

The chapter on the Chinese-Japanese connection breaks down into five main sections: 1. China, Japan and the West; 2. The Impact of the First World War on Sino-Japanese Relations; 3. Japanese Designs on China; 4. The Japanese Occupation of Manchuria; 5. China and Japan at War. Each of these themes raises questions which are central to an examination of Sino-Japanese relations.

1 China, Japan and the West

Key question: Why had China been unable to modernise itself with the same degree of success as Japan?

Section 1 of this chapter is required reading and also sections 1-3 of Chapter 1.

Points to consider: The impact of Western imperialism on China and Japan was profound. How the two countries reacted to their subordination to the West determined their subsequent development as nations. Therefore, the critical question to ask is why Japan's reaction was so different from China's. The basic answer is that Japan was capable of responding as a united nation; China was not. The explanation for this must lie in a consideration of the geographical, administrative, political and social differences between them. The compact nature of Japan geographically made it much easier for its government to reshape its social structure and modernise its economy. The sheer size of China made such developments so much more difficult to organise effectively. It would be advisable at this point to re-examine the description of China in Chapter 1. The Chinese found it extremely hard to throw off millennia of tradition; there was an inertia about their political system that prevented their easy adaptation to new ways. In contrast, Japan began to modernise itself with remarkable speed and effectiveness. Some historians have suggested that this was unnatural, that it was an enforced grafting rather than an organic growth. Japan, they argue, deliberately Europeanised itself in pursuit of two main objectives: the creation of an industrial economy and the formation of a powerful army and navy. These were achieved, but only at the cost of an institutional rigidity, which destroyed individualism and left Japan prey to militarism. These are the points worth bearing in mind when analysing the reasons for the disparity between China and Japan in this period.

2 The Impact of the First World War on Sino-Japanese Relations

Key question: 'Despite its apparent gains at the expense of its neighbour, Japan had more reason than China to feel betrayed at the outcome of the First World War.' Discuss.

Section 2 of this chapter is required reading, but also look at sections 2 and 3 of Chapter 2, and section 4 of chapter 4.

Points to consider: To understand the involvement of China and Japan in the 1914-18 war requires an appreciation of both the domestic situation in China and the attitude of the Western powers towards the Far East. It is important, therefore, to make the relevant cross references to Chapters 2 and 4. The Sino-Japanese reaction to the war in Europe emphasised the wide gap in strength and aspiration between Japan and China. Key questions that present themselves are why Japan was able to tighten the screw on China, as evident in the 21 Demands, and why the Chinese leaders, albeit reluctantly, accepted this humiliation. The end of the war marked a further humiliation for the Chinese; they received nothing for their efforts and the scant regard that the Versailles delegates showed towards them was a clear mark of the low esteem in which China was held internationally. Neither China nor Japan was satisfied by the outcome of the war and the peace settlement that followed. Ostensibly Japan was a beneficiary; it obtained the territories it claimed. But in the postwar period it felt betrayed by the USA's protectionist economic policies and by the explicit racism of US immigration laws. It is interesting to reflect that it had been the USA who had blocked a clause submitted by Japan that the terms of the peace settlement should include the international acceptance of the principle of racial equality. Such dismissive treatment intensified Japan's desire for self-assertion. China was the immediate victim.

3 Japanese Designs on China

Key question: Consider the view that Japan's aggressive intentions towards China were a product not of militarism but of economic necessity.

Sections 2 and 3 of this chapter are required reading, also sections 5 and 6 of Chapter 4.

Points to consider: This is the central theme that links all five topics in this chapter. The study of the character of Japan's designs is very closely related to the preceding section. China had obvious strategic and economic attractions for the Japanese. The question that arises is whether, given their shared humiliation at the hands of the West, the two Far Eastern neighbours could work in harmony and present a common front against the rest of the world. That, of course, is what Japan claimed to be aiming for in proposing the East Asian Co-Prosperity Sphere. But the further question arises concerning the sincerity of the Japanese call for unity. Did not their traditional animosity and their recent financial exploitation of China mean that there was never a possibility of real co-operation? Certainly, the severity of their occupation of China, beginning with Manchuria in 1931, hardly suggests that the Japanese regarded the Chinese as worthy of equal consideration. The viewpoint that deserves most attention is that Japanese aggression towards China, far from being gratuitous, arose from a very real fear that unless it had the resources of China at its disposal Japan could not sustain itself as a nation.

4 The Japanese Occupation of Manchuria

Key question: Did the Japanese occupation of Manchuria in 1931 end any possibility of genuine co-operation between China and Japan?

Section 3 and 4 of this chapter and sections 5 and 6 of Chapter 4 are required reading.

Points to consider. Manchuria was regarded by the Japanese as having a critical place in their commerce and strategy. It was necessary, ran the Japanese argument, that the area be occupied before the USSR seized it as a base from which to threaten the Japanese mainland. What complicates the picture is that within Japan's governing circles there was a marked lack of unanimity over the issue. The government and military were at variance and there was a sharp divergence between the main branches of the armed services. Was the occupation of Manchuria, therefore, a logical development of an anxious Japan's genuine concern for its national survival or was it a local military initiative that obliged the Japanese civilian government to embark on a course of action which it had not originally intended? Equally important to consider is the evident willingness of numbers of prominent Chinese to co-operate with the occupiers in the creation of client states. This does suggest that the idea of collaboration with Japan was not universally regarded in China as betrayal. It adds weight to the Japanese notion of China and Japan acting together. In hindsight, there seems to have been little chance of genuine Sino-Japanese co-operation; this is because we are aware of the mutual bitterness that was to develop over fourteen years of conflict. But is this to say that there was never a real possibility of China reaching reasonable terms with their occupiers in an anti-Western front?

5 China and Japan at War

Key question: Examine the contention that 'the Sino-Japanese War of 1937-45 led Chiang Kaishek down a political blind alley'.

Reading: sections 4 and 5 of this chapter are required reading, also sections 2 to 4 of Chapter 3, and section 7 of Chapter 4.

Points to consider: One school of thought argues that the Xian agreement of 1936 made an extension of the Japanese occupation into a full-scale war inevitable. The CCP-GMD United Front had pledged itself to drive the Japanese from China, a pledge that necessarily ruled out co-operation with the occupier. However, it was also the case that Chiang Kaishek's commitment to the Front was far from total. His basic aim was to destroy the Communists; until that was achieved he followed a flexible policy that often seemed to veer towards accommodation with the Japanese. There are grounds for suggesting that, but for the Xian commitment, he would not have entertained open confrontation with the Japanese armies. It has also to be borne in mind that, as in 1931, so in 1937 it was a Japanese move which began the war. Whether the Chinese on their own could survive the full weight of the Japanese armies became an academic point once Japan had chosen to make war on the USA in 1941. Chiang's elation at the news of Pearl Harbor was understandable; the Nationalist cause was now inextricably linked with the fate of the Allies in the Pacific war. What he could not foresee was the extraordinary way in which the war would end. The dramatic and sudden climax of the war in 1945 destroyed the expectations which had sustained him since 1937. There were no massive landings of American troops on the Chinese mainland; the Communists were not rolled up with the Japanese. Instead Chiang was left facing a CCP army which, while numerically weaker than his own, was superior as a fighting force as its resistance to the Japanese had already shown. The war which earlier had seemed to be the means by which Chiang would consolidate his power in China had finally betrayed him militarily and politically.

Source analysis on 'China and Japan'

The following is an analysis of the 21 Demands of 1915, a major document concerning Sino-Soviet relations that appears on page 96.

1 - Context

The 21 Demands were officially delivered in 1915 by Japan to the republican government of Yuan Shikai. The Japanese had used the opportunity provided by the confusion and weakness of the 1912 Republic and the preoccupation of the Western powers with the war in Europe to increase its dominance over China.

2 - Meaning

The 21 Demands list the concessions Japan requires from China. The reference to German-held Shandong introduces a key province whose strategic value made it of particular interest to Japan, which demands that in any subsequent Japanese-German agreement China will recognise Japan's full rights over the area. A similar demand is made in regard to Manchuria and Mongolia; Japanese nationals are to be entitled to full civil and commercial rights in those provinces, and the Chinese are required to accept Japanese political, military and economic advisers in China at large. Specified Chinese companies are not to augment or dispose of their assets unless this has been sanctioned by Japan. The Chinese have also to acquiesce in Japanese control of their police forces. In financial matters, the Chinese are not free to negotiate foreign loans without first receiving Japan's permission. A similar restriction lays down that no less than half the military hardware needed by China is to be purchased from Japan. Even religion comes within the range of the demands; the Japanese are to be granted the freedom to send Buddhist missionaries to China.

3 - Significance

This document is central to an understanding of Sino-Japanese relations in the first half of the twentieth century. Had the 21 Demands been fully implemented, China's status as a sovereign state would have been totally compromised. This was indeed Japan's objective. Its intention of controlling China's economic, military and cultural life is clearly evident. Japan had seized the moment provided by the war in Europe to extend the hold on China that it had been developing since the 1890s. One of the main areas of debate among scholars is whether China and Japan, given their historical animosity, were permanently locked in rivalry or whether their geographical location and economic needs were compelling reasons for their forming a common east-Asian front as a mutual protection in a hostile world.

Evidence such as this source strongly suggests that Japan's designs on China were basically expansionist and aggressive. It is instructive to compare this extract with the Tanaka Memorial on page 99. The two sources are complementary in that they show the character of Japan's demands and the motives behind them. Japan feared that unless it gained control of the Chinese economy and of key provinces, such as Manchuria, it could not sustain itself as a modern nation. Japanese aggression towards China was, therefore, the norm; later proposals that the two nations should work together appear more often to be expedient ruses on Japan's part rather than a genuine appeal for co-operation. It is also highly significant that Yuan, who was seeking to ingratiate himself with the Japanese, bowed to the 21 Demands. His surrender created a violent reaction among the Chinese, the first example of the determined anti-Japanese resistance that was to develop over the next thirty years, reaching its climax in the Chinese victory of 1945.

CHAPTER 6

China and the Soviet Union

1 Marxism Comes to China

There was much about Russia that appealed to China's revolutionaries and reformers in the early twentieth century. In terms of their recent history and current circumstance, there was a striking similarity between the two countries. Both had recently been defeated by Japan, both were trying to come to terms with the need for economic and political modernisation, and both were poor relations when compared with the advanced, wealth producing, nations of western Europe and the USA. This fellow feeling towards Russia was intensified when the Chinese learned of the Bolshevik success in the 1917 revolution. Chinese intellectuals wrote admiringly in 1918 of the achievements of Lenin and the Bolsheviks in throwing off the slough of history by ridding themselves of tsarist oppression and establishing a workers' state. Admiration increased when the Chinese learned of the Red Army's defeat of the foreign interventionists in Russia in the period 1918-20. Here was a living example of the overthrow of Western imperialism, made more impressive by the fact that the nations whom the Bolsheviks had repelled were the very same as those currently occupying China. This was successful anti-imperialism in action.

Historians frequently allude to the years 1900-25 as marking an 'intellectual revolution' in China, a reference to the quickening of interest in those Western philosophies and political theories that might offer a solution to China's besetting problems. The University of Beijing became the centre of this renaissance. Chen Duzui and Li Dazhao (Li Ta-chao), leading academics at the University, encouraged their students to challenge the Confucian-dominated ideas of traditional Chinese scholarship. This was not simply an intellectual pursuit. Indeed, save for a few scholars, pure theory was not particularly attractive to the Chinese. They were looking for practical answers to real problems. A specific political theory was appealing to the Chinese only insofar as it could be applied in the real world. This is an aspect of the utilitarian approach that has long been a characteristic of Chinese politics. The common feature of Chinese revolutionaries was their rejection of the decadent system that had failed China and had allowed foreigners to impose themselves on the nation. What they were seeking was a programme that would offer a solution to China's ills. The revolutionary movements at this time, whether of the right or of the left, were essentially nationalistic. They were all driven by a desire for Chinese regeneration.

The revolutionary ideas of Karl Marx had been known in China since the beginning of the century, but what gave them special relevance and appeal was the apparent failure of the 1911 revolution and of the

Republic that followed to advance China's cause. Disillusioned Chinese radicals turned impatiently away from what they regarded as the failure of democracy in China. They were drawn instead to another Western philosophy, but this time one that had been rejected by the West. The fear and detestation with which the imperialist nations regarded Marxism gave it an added attraction for the Chinese. To the young intellectuals who came together to form the Chinese Communist Party in the early 1920s, the great inspiration, therefore, was the successful October Revolution in Russia in 1917. They could now observe a Marxist state in action; anti-imperialism and anti-capitalism now had a national home. The rejection of Western values, implicit in the Bolshevik Revolution, appealed greatly to Chinese revolutionaries for whom the main attraction of Marxism-Leninism was its explanation of the capitalist phase of imperialism, the process which had led to China's current humiliation at Western hands. When one of the first actions of the new Soviet state proved to be the renunciation of Russia's traditional claim to Chinese territories, the respect of revolutionaries in China for the Bolsheviks knew no bounds.

The Bolshevik government was eager to turn this to advantage. The failure of revolution to make headway elsewhere in Europe encouraged the Bolsheviks to turn their attention to the colonial areas. The unstable situation in China, which to Russian eyes looked ready for revolution, led the new Soviet state to make immediate contact with the Chinese Marxists. One of the first moves of the Comintern, set up in Moscow in 1919 by the Bolshevik government as the principal organisation for fomenting international revolution, was to send agents to China and other regions under Western colonial control. Lenin's interpretation of imperialism became especially relevant at this point. The Bolshevik leader's main argument was that Western colonialism marked a definite predetermined phase in the revolutionary dialectical process. As capitalism began to strangle itself through over-production and competition for declining home markets, it sought to survive by exploiting overseas territories, either as dumping grounds for surplus produce or as sources of cheap raw material and labour. Imperialism was thus an expression of capitalism in crisis. It followed that the historical role of the exploited colonial peoples was to rise up against their oppressors so as to achieve not only their own liberation but also the collapse of international capitalism. In 1918 Joseph Stalin, the Bolshevik Commissar for Nationalities, gave exact expression to the Soviet concept of imperialism as it applied to China:

1 The imperialists view the East as the fountain of their happiness because it contains an unaccountable amount of natural resources such as cotton, petroleum, gold, coal, and iron ore. In view of its wealth, is the East not the imperialists' 'sweetest fruit'? While they
5 are fighting and making a mess of Europe, they are constantly

thinking of such countries as China, India, Persia, Egypt, and Morocco. In fact, they fight precisely because they wish to control the East. We can readily understand why they are so enthusiastic to maintain 'legitimacy and order' in the Eastern countries because without 'legitimacy and order' they would not be able to continue
10 to control these remote areas.

The imperialists want not only the East's natural resources but also its 'obedient' people, the 'cheap' Oriental manpower which they can utilize for their own selfish purposes. They wish to recruit from these 'obedient' people enough 'boys' to form the so-called
15 'coloured' army and to use this army to crush their own revolutionary workers at home. This is the reason they call their Eastern colonies and semicolonies 'inexhaustible' manpower reserves.

The purpose of us Communists is to wake up the oppressed
20 Oriental peoples from their one hundred years' slumber and to imbue their workers and peasants with a revolutionary spirit to conduct an uncompromising struggle against the imperialists. Our goal is to take away from these imperialists their 'most dependable' rear areas and their 'inexhaustible' manpower resources. Without a
25 struggle of this nature there will not be any final victory for socialism; nor can our battle against the imperialists be completely successful.

For the first time in history the Russian Revolution has aroused the oppressed peoples in the East to struggle against the imperialists.

The Marxist-Leninist theory of imperialism offered the Chinese both an explanation of why they had been humiliated by the West and a means of restoring their former greatness. In October 1920 Lenin declared to a Chinese delegation visiting Moscow, 'The Chinese revolution will finally cause the downfall of world imperialism'. Lenin's concepts became the orthodoxy which determined the Soviet approach to colonial struggles. However, although this was not realised at first, his ideas contained a basic flaw which was permanently to distort Soviet Russia's relations with revolutionary China. Lenin equated the movements for national liberation from colonialism with the struggle of the industrial proletariat against capitalism. The weakness of this idea was that in few countries did the stage of social and economic development fit the dialectical theory. It certainly did not apply in China which had yet to develop a genuine proletariat; in an overwhelmingly rural population of 500 million, scarcely 3 million could be classified as industrial workers. If China was to experience a popular revolution, it would have to come from the peasants in the countryside. Yet the Comintern, committed to the concept of proletarian revolution, was to persist throughout its twenty-four years of activity in China (1919-43) in instructing the CCP to develop as an urban party and plan urban revolution.

However, these anomalies lay in the future. In the early 'twenties the relations between Moscow and the Chinese were cordial. Two Comintern agents, Voitinsky and Maring, were instrumental in the formal setting up of the Chinese Communist Party (CCP) in July 1921. Twenty representatives from various provinces gathered in Shanghai to adopt a basic revolutionary programme and elect an executive committee. Chen Duziu became the Secretary General. Of equal significance was the presence of Chen's protégé from Beijing, Mao Zedong, who represented Hunan province. Although a tiny party numerically, containing only 50 members in 1921, the CCP had some success during the next two years in organising strikes and boycotts in Shanghai and Hong Kong. However, its attempt in 1923 to organise a railway strike in the Beijing region, an area under the control of the warlord Wu Peifu, proved wholly unsuccessful.

2 The GMD-CCP United Front

It was the CCP's ineffectiveness in the face of warlord power that convinced the Comintern that the Communists were incapable of being a genuinely revolutionary force on their own. The way forward, it argued, was for the CCP to ally itself with the other major revolutionary party in China, the Guomindang. The Comintern urged the young Communist Party to co-operate with Sun Yatsen, whose brand of socialism it interpreted as very much akin to Marxism. In 1923, the Comintern agents, Adolf Joffe and Michael Borodin, made direct contact with the GMD, offering to assist with money and military supplies. The immediate outcome was a pact of friendship between Moscow and the GMD. This prompted the Comintern advisers in China to renew their call to the CCP to throw in their lot with the Nationalists in advancing a broad-front revolutionary force in China. For his part, Sun Yatsen was very willing to respond to Moscow's overtures. Confronted by powerful warlords, his GMD government in Guangzhou was finding it extremely difficult to make good its claim to authority in southern China. Furthermore, Sun genuinely admired the structure and discipline of the Russian Bolshevik Party. He saw common ground between their revolutionary programme and his own Three People's Principles. He accepted the requests of the Comintern that the members of the young CCP should be allowed to join the GMD, though he required that they did so as individuals rather than as a Communist bloc. By allowing the CCP to keep its separate identity, Sun hoped to keep Moscow contented enough for it to continue supplying the GMD with money and ammunition.

Initially, a majority of the Chinese Communists believed that a common front between themselves and the Nationalists was the best means both of destroying the warlords and expelling the foreigners, aims which were fundamental to all revolutionaries. It is important to stress that the CCP and GMD were both revolutionary parties. The Nationalists under Chiang Kaishek would later come to be regarded as essentially reactionary, but we must not lose sight of how progressive many of them originally were. That is certainly how they were seen by Moscow, which eased the path to closer co-operation with the GMD by acknowledging that the creation of a soviet system was not immediately necessary in China; the priority for revolution was national unity against the imperialists. This view was formally adopted as party policy by the CCP at both its second and third congresses in 1922 and 1923 when it voted for union with the GMD:

1 In the absence of a strong proletarian class, it is natural that there cannot be a strong Communist Party, a party of the masses to meet the demands of the forthcoming revolution. Therefore, the Communist International has decided that the Chinese Commun-
5 ist Party should co-operate with the Guomindang and that the Chinese Communists should join the Guomindang as individuals.
   We shall preserve our own organization after we have joined the Guomindang. Moreover, we shall do our utmost to attract to our party revolutionary elements of true class consciousness from the
10 Guomindang leftists as well as members of labour organizations. The purpose is to gradually expand our organization and to strictly enforce our party discipline so that the foundation of a strong Communist Party with mass followings will be eventually established ....
15   We should strive to expand the Guomindang organization to all parts of China and gather all the revolutionary elements under the Guomindang banner in order to meet today's revolutionary demand. Even though the political struggle we are waging today is merely a people's movement, the movement of expelling foreign
20 power from China and eliminating warlords within, we should nevertheless conduct intensive propaganda among the labouring masses so as to broaden the basis of the revolutionary Guomindang and emphasize the necessity of supporting the proletariat's interest in the people's movement ....
25   The small capitalist class we have in China will quickly develop and become strong after the success of the democratic revolution, and it will certainly take a position opposite to that of the proletarian class. Then we proletarians must deal with the capitalist class and proceed with the second stage of our struggle,
30 namely, the establishment of a proletarian dictatorship based on an alliance between workers and poor peasants ...

Yet, even at this early stage, there were those in the CCP who were uneasy at the thought of a merger along the lines advocated by the Comintern. Chen Duziu was concerned that the Russian advice derived from an incomplete reading of the situation in China. He considered that the aims of the GMD were too imprecise for it to be accepted as a truly revolutionary force and he was disturbed that so many of the GMD's members came from the bourgeois elements of China's east-coast cities. The Comintern agents made light of Chen's anxieties. They assured him that the GMD was dominated not by the bourgeoisie but by pro-Moscow Marxist sympathisers and that what brought the various Chinese revolutionary forces together, hatred of warlordism and foreign imperialists, was more important than anything that might divide them. The Comintern repeated its instruction to join the Nationalists. Overawed by the reputation of the Russian Bolsheviks as the leaders of world revolution, most CCP members swallowed their misgivings and did as they were told.

3 China's Place in Soviet Foreign Policy

The Comintern calculated that when their respective size and influence were taken into consideration, the GMD stood far more chance than the CCP of achieving real power in China. Comintern reports to the Kremlin consistently took the line that, since the CCP was too small to produce a revolution on its own, it should be directed to work with the GMD in a broad movement of the Chinese left. Ironically, this had a marked resemblance to the view of the Mensheviks in Russia before 1917, who had urged the formation of a broad-front revolutionary movement. This had been violently rejected by the Bolsheviks. Nonetheless, the Kremlin now found it expedient to pursue this line in China.

The USSR's attitude towards the Chinese situation needs to be understood in relation to its broader international concerns. Feeling vulnerable in a hostile world, the Soviet Union was concerned to safeguard its Far Eastern frontiers. Co-operation with the GMD was more likely to secure Russian interests in Mongolia and thus preserve it as a buffer against the growing strength of Japan. It was such thinking that lay behind the USSR's seizure of Outer Mongolia in 1924 and its insistence that the Beijing government recognise its right to retain hold of the Chinese Eastern Railway, which provided the trans-Siberian railway with a short cut to its Pacific terminus. These moves were clear evidence that when it came to a question of its own national concerns Soviet Russia was less than wholly committed to the proletarian principle it had proclaimed in 1918 of abandoning all claims to foreign territory.

In some respects, political divisions within China suited the USSR, which had been willing initially to give aid to some of the stronger warlords, General Feng in northern China being an example. The

Comintern had even considered encouraging the CCP to ally with the more powerful warlords, but it subsequently saw greater prospects in urging an alliance with the Nationalists. The Comintern's belief that the revolutionary future lay with the Nationalists was shown by the efforts it put into reorganising the GMD along Soviet lines. In 1924, Borodin played a major role in drafting a new GMD constitution, which, out of deference to Sun Yatsen was nominally based on the Three People's Principles, but which was clearly Leninist in character. In keeping with Lenin's concept of democratic centralism, power was to be concentrated in the hands of the leaders and great emphasis was placed on the need for an effective GMD army. The Red Army had been the saviour of Bolshevism in the Russian Civil War (1918-20). The Comintern argued that without a similar military organisation the Chinese revolutionaries would be incapable of overcoming either the warlords or the imperialist occupiers.

The outcome of all this was the formation of the GMD-CCP United Front, pledged to the furtherance of revolution whose next stage would be the destruction of the warlords. Since this required the formation of a powerful army, the chief beneficiaries were the Nationalists, who were now led by Chiang Kaishek, following the death of Sun Yatsen in March 1925. The elevation of Chiang, who had been the commander of the GMD's army headquarters in Guangzhou, meant that the balance within the party had shifted very much towards the military wing. From this point onwards military considerations tended to take precedence over purely political ones in the GMD's policies. There was a logic to this. If China wished to enjoy genuine political independence it would have first to free itself of warlordism and foreign control. This could be done only by force of arms. Neither the warlords nor the imperialists were likely to be moved by any other argument. From their southern base, the GMD declared a national crusade against the warlords and called upon all true revolutionaries to join them in the 'Northern Expedition'.

After initial misgivings, the CCP, which had been co-operating since 1923 with the Nationalists in a number of provinces, accepted the instructions of their Comintern advisers and joined the expedition. In doing so they played into Chiang Kaishek's hands; Chiang wanted CCP support only in order to break the warlords. His ulterior motive was to destroy the Communists themselves. Once it became evident that the expedition had realised its first aim of subduing the warlords, Chiang duly turned on his CCP allies in the White Terror of 1927 (see page 37) and very nearly annihilated them. There were attempts at CCP resistance, the most notable being the Autumn Harvest rising led by Mao Zedong in Hunan province in September 1927. The Rising was intended as more than just a military action. It was an assertion of the CCP's independence and therefore a deliberate defiance of Moscow's order that, despite the White Terror, the United Front must be maintained. However, the rising failed and the CCP appeared to be on the point of being overwhelmed. That the Communists survived at all was because a contingent of them rejected the Comintern's orders and fled to the mountains of Jiangxi province. Mao Zedong was one of those who led the break away.

Between 1924 and 1927 the GMD and the CCP, under Soviet tutelage, had maintained an uneasy but effective front against the warlords. This alliance had now been dramatically riven by Chiang's uncompromising moves. The vital question arose: how would the Soviet Union respond to this threat to the continued existence of Marxism in China?

4 Stalin and Mao

Under Stalin, who had emerged as the Soviet leader by 1927, the USSR's concern was always to safeguard its own position. At this stage, it had no wish to antagonise Japan over the Manchurian border question, and it was worried that the Western powers might use the occasion of the Northern Expedition to interfere directly in Chinese affairs. What is noticeable is that under Stalin the USSR was far more anxious to protect its diplomatic interests nationally than it was to act as a spur to international revolution. A chief reason why the Comintern was never an effective body was that, despite its belligerent propaganda, its programme invariably came second to the USSR's national concerns. It is striking how conservative Soviet policy could be in defence of its own interests. Right up to the Shanghai massacre, Stalin maintained the fiction that the GMD was working ultimately for a socialist revolution. When it became apparent that Chiang Kaishek's intention of destroying the Communists was in deadly earnest, Stalin attempted to save face by encouraging a Communist rising in Guangzhou, which in the event proved a complete failure. Yet he still declined to reverse his basic policy.

This was not simply a matter of ideology. The power struggle in Russia among the Bolsheviks' leaders was more significant in shaping Soviet policy than what was happening in China. Indeed, the policy towards China has to be seen as an aspect of the leadership contest between Stalin and Trotsky that followed the death of Lenin in 1924. When Trotsky belatedly realised that the Comintern, by insisting on the maintenance of the United Front, was acquiescing in the destruction of Chinese Communism he made desperate attempts to force the Politburo to change the policy. Seeing Trotsky's move as part of a power bid, Stalin resisted and a bitter dispute followed. The very fact that Trotsky demanded a policy shift towards China meant, in the nature of Bolshevik power struggles, that his opponents would become even more resolute in not shifting. Instead, Stalin and his supporters produced dialectical justifications for their pro-Nationalist, anti-Communist, line.

Their argument was essentially that China, being at a backward stage of the class war, had first to undergo a bourgeois revolution before it could progress to the proletarian phase. Stalin asserted that there were three main elements making up the GMD: the advanced bourgeoisie, the petty bourgeoisie and the masses. In the historical circumstances in which China found herself, it was essential that the advanced bourgeoisie be supported. Since it was they who held the reins of power, it would be by way of a bourgeois rising that China would move to its ultimate socialist revolution. At this stage in history, therefore, the bourgeois Nationalists were the real revolutionaries in China and were to be supported even at the expense of the CCP.

Events gave increasing substance to Trotsky's charge that Stalin was 'the grave-digger of the Chinese Revolution'. Stalin seemed prepared to sacrifice the CCP to the interests of the Soviet Union. Even during the period from 1927 to 1934 when Chiang Kaishek was systematically choking the CCP in its Jiangxi mountain base, Stalin persisted in the discredited policy of maintaining the United Front. He refused to believe, then and after, that the Chinese Communists were capable, by themselves, of taking power in China. Right down to October 1949 when the Chinese People's Republic was established, Stalin continued to support the Nationalists in the belief that they would prove the ultimate victors.

Mao Zedong, who had risen to prominence in the CCP as a result of his highly effective propaganda work in Hunan province in the 1920s, had reached the same conclusion as Trotsky, that Stalin was an enemy of the CCP's real interests. By the mid 1920s Mao had come to the realisation that if a genuine people's revolution was to be accomplished it would have to be a rising of the peasantry. China was a predominantly rural society, 80 per cent of the population being peasants. For Mao, a slavish adherence to the Marxist theory of proletarian revolution made no sense for China; its revolution had to be peasant-based. Even after Chiang Kaishek had launched his extermination campaign against the Communists, many CCP members loyally obeyed the Comintern's instructions to maintain the alliance with the GMD and went to their inevitable doom. Not so, Mao Zedong; carrying with him an abiding distaste for Stalin and Bolshevism, Mao took to the hills of Jiangxi province, there between 1927 and 1934 to develop a brand of Chinese communism free from Russian taint. This explains why he was always prepared to modify Marxist theory if it did not suit the Chinese context. This, in turn, is the explanation for the strained relations between Mao and the Kremlin that persisted throughout his career. Mao was never willing to allow Stalin and the Soviet leaders to dictate the nature and pace of Chinese communism.

5 Sino-Soviet Tensions, 1935-45

Throughout the years 1935-45, Mao and his followers were able to develop political propaganda techniques aimed at winning over the peasants and convincing them that the Communists were the true defenders of China against Japanese aggression. They received no help from the USSR in their resistance to the invader. The policy of the Soviet Union towards Japan in the 1930s was circumspect and low key. It did have long-term designs in the Far East and its contiguous border with China made it especially sensitive to Japanese expansionism. However, such concerns had to take second place to its greater fears for its western borders. The Soviet Union was not uninterested in the Far-Eastern question. It was simply preoccupied elsewhere. Although in Europe in the 1930s it sought to create anti-German alliances in order to protect its western borders, it followed no such policy in the Far East. The Soviet government under Stalin believed that it could best serve both the Communist cause and its own territorial aims by pursuing a unilateral policy towards China.

It was not merely that the USSR declined to assist the Chinese Communists. Cut off from close contact with the CCP, it continued to give its support throughout the 1930s to Chiang Kaishek and the Nationalists. Stalin's hope was that by encouraging GMD resistance to the Japanese occupation of China that began in earnest in 1937, Russia would then be less likely itself to be the object of Japanese aggression. Broadly, this policy worked. There were a series of Russo-Japanese incidents in the late 1930s that led to fighting on the Manchurian border, but these were resolved in 1941 with the signing of a non-aggression pact between the Soviet Union and Japan. This held good until August 1945 when, in keeping with a commitment given to the Allies at Yalta in February 1945, the USSR declared war on Japan only days before the Japanese surrender in August of that year.

After the Long March and the establishment of the Chinese Soviet base at Yanan, the USSR and the Comintern ceased to have any real influence upon the development of Chinese communism. This was what reduced Stalin to disparaging Mao's followers as being Communists only in name; 'they are "white" at heart, even though they wear "red" jackets'. It was the memory of such dismissive treatment that so angered Mao after 1949 when Stalin attempted to claim that the establishment of the Chinese People's Republic owed as much to the moral leadership and example of the USSR as it did to the CCP's own efforts. Mao could justly claim that his party had survived twenty-five years of civil war and fifteen years of Japanese occupation without help from the Soviet Union. Indeed, had Soviet advice been followed, there would not have been a viable Chinese Communist Party.

One extraordinary incident indicates the degree of antipathy between Mao and Stalin. This relates to the launching of Germany's Barbarossa campaign against the USSR on 22 June 1941. Two days before the attack, Zhou Enlai, who had received his information via the GMD's anti-Japanese spy network, sent precise details of the German invasion plans to the Kremlin. These were acknowledged by Molotov but Stalin declined to act upon them, since this would have been to admit the failure of the whole of his diplomacy towards Germany since the Nazi-Soviet Pact of 1939. The Russian leader's refusal to face reality in June 1941 very nearly destroyed him and the USSR. Although he subsequently recovered his nerve and became an outstanding war leader, Stalin, in the eyes of Mao and the Chinese Communists, was never again to be fully trusted as a revolutionary. It is true that there would be intermittent rapprochements between the Kremlin and the CCP, but these were never to develop into a genuine understanding or a joint sense of purpose.

That is why Stalin's decision in 1943 to dissolve the Comintern should not be interpreted as a concession to Chinese Communist sensitivities. This apparently remarkable move has to be seen as a part of Second World War diplomacy; it was meant to impress Russia's ally, the USA. Nevertheless, there are grounds for regarding it as a tacit admission by the USSR that it was incapable of directly shaping Chinese Communism. Mao's description of why the Comintern had become redundant in China is instructive. *The Liberation Daily* reported a speech he gave to the CCP at Yanan in which he spelled out the reasons why the Comintern had to be dissolved.

1 First, correct leadership should be based upon careful, detailed study of local conditions which can only be done by each of the Communist parties in its own country. The Comintern, far away from the actual struggle, can no longer provide proper leadership.
5 Second, in the anti-Fascist struggle it has been long felt that a centralized international organization is no longer adequate to meet the fast-changing situation.
    Third, the leadership in each of the world's Communist parties has grown steadily and has become politically more mature.
10 Comrade Mao cited the CCP as an example. The CCP has undergone three revolutionary movements, all of which are continuous and extremely complicated, much more complicated than the Russian Revolution. From these movements the CCP has created its own experienced, veteran cadres of the finest quality.
15 Since 1935 when the Comintern held its Seventh Congress, it has never interfered with the CCP's policies or decisions. Yet the CCP has done exceptionally well in waging a liberation warfare against the Japanese aggression.
    Comrade Mao also pointed out that revolutionary movement
20 can be neither exported nor imported. Though the CCP has received assistance from the Comintern, its birth and development

result primarily from the political awakening of the Chinese
proletariat. In other words, it is the Chinese proletariat who have
created and developed the Chinese Communist Party. Though the
25 CCP has a history of only twenty-two years, it has undergone three
great revolutionary movements.
    The principle of Marxism-Leninism dictates that the organiza-
tional form of a revolution should be subservient to the practical
need of the revolution. If an organizational form is no longer
30 compatible with the practical need of the revolution, it should of
course be abolished.

Essentially what Mao was saying was that the hegemony of the USSR in
international Communism was no longer appropriate. China's Communist revolution would be run on Chinese not Russian lines. It was an
assertion of Chinese independence and provided a fitting commentary
on twenty years of increasing Sino-Soviet estrangement.

6 The Failure of Sino-Soviet Relations, 1945-9

The low estimation in which Moscow held Mao and the CCP was
revealed in August 1945 when the Soviet Union formally signed a
Treaty of Friendship with Chiang Kaishek's Nationalist government.
The Treaty declared that its terms ended 'all outstanding grievances'
between China and the USSR. The British newspaper, The *Observer*,
commented on the significance of the Soviet Union's abandonment of
the Chinese Communists:

> The cynic may be inclined to regard Russia's part in the conclusion
> of the treaty with China as a sacrifice of the Yenan regime for the
> sake of greater prestige and influence in Chungking and hence over
> all China.

Hindsight has shown the accuracy of the *Observer's* assessment. It can
now be appreciated that the Friendship Treaty was of a diplomatic piece
with the Soviet Union's declaration of war on Japan in August 1945 in
the last days of the conflict in China. The USSR was manoeuvring itself
into a position from which it could seize Chinese territory. Soviet armies
occupied Manchuria between August 1945 and May 1946 and did not
withdraw until they had stripped the region of its economic resources.
The Soviet booty was calculated at $2 billion. Anything that could be
transported was taken. There were even stories of cooling towers being
cut in half and loaded on to Russian trains.
    The upshot of this was that, when the Japanese grip on China was
broken and the GMD-CCP civil war was resumed, the USSR remained
a largely impotent onlooker. It made some gestures of goodwill towards
Mao Zedong and the Kremlin continued to send its representatives to

CCP gatherings, but, even when the Red Army began to drive the Nationalists from their bases, Stalin could not bring himself to change tack. As late as 1949 the year in which the Reds forced the GMD off the Chinese mainla d, the USSR persisted in recognising Chiang Kaishek as China's leader. Stalin appeared to have believed throughout this period that the USA would not tolerate a Communist victory in China. Anxious not to provoke further American intervention in the Far East, he urged Mao to come to terms with the Nationalists, even if this meant accepting a China divided between the Reds in the north and the GMD in the south. Mao later recorded:

1 Even in 1949 when we were about to cross the Yangtze River, *someone* [Stalin] still wanted to prevent us. According to him we should under no circumstances cross the Yangtze. If we did so America would send troops to China and become directly involved 5 in China's Civil War and the South and North dynasties would reappear in China.
    I did not listen to what [he] said. We crossed the Yangtze. America did not send troops and there were no South and North dynasties. If we really had followed his words surely there would be 10 a situation of South and North dynasties.

That not only the USA but also the Soviet Union had continued to support the GMD until almost the last moment confirmed Mao Zedong in his long-held belief that salvation for China was possible only from within China itself. The unfolding of events he read as a justification for the independent Marxist line that he had taken since the mid 1920s. By 1949 he was more than ever convinced that for China the Chinese way was the only way. All of which supports the conclusion that, given the different national, cultural, and ideological standpoints from which they started, there had never been a real likelihood that the revolutionaries of the USSR and China would come to share a common purpose and vision.

Studying 'China and the Soviet Union'

The chapter on Sino-Soviet relations divides into five main sections: 1. The impact of Marxism on China; 2. China's place in Soviet foreign policy; 3. The relations between Stalin and Mao Zedong; 4. Sino-Soviet tensions, 1935-45; 5. The breakdown of Sino-Soviet relations, 1945-9. Each of these themes raises questions which are central to an examination of relations between China and the Soviet Union.

The appeal of Marxism-Leninism to the Chinese

China's 'intellectual revolution'
China and Russia at a similar stage of history
the failure of China's 1911 revolution
the success of the Bolshevik Revolution
Lenin's interpretation of imperialism

The formation of the CCP

the University of Beijing
challenge to Confucianism
anti-colonialism
Chen Duzui and Li Dazhao
Mao Zedong
the role of the Comintern

The CCP goes its own way

rejects Comintern orders
abandons the United Front
the Jianxi Soviet
the Long March
the Yanan Soviet

Conflicting concepts of revolution

Stalin ←—————→ Mao Zedong

Stalin	Mao Zedong
urban	rural
industrial workers	peasants
committed to GMD	primacy of the CCP
Soviet interests paramount	Chinese interests paramount

Sino-Soviet Tensions, 1935-49

Stalin - 'the grave-digger of the Chinese Revolution'
Mao's rejection of Soviet hegemony
'revolution can be neither exported nor imported'
the USSR continued to support Chiang and the GMD

Summary - China and the Soviet Union

1. The impact of Marxism on China

Key question: Why were Chinese revolutionaries so attracted to Marxist theories?

Section 1 of this chapter and sections 1 and 2 of Chapter 1 are required reading.

Points to consider: An essential point to stress is that pure theory seldom attracted Chinese political thinkers. Ideas were valued in accordance with their value as practical guides. It is unlikely that Marxism would have made the impact it did without the example of a successful Marxist revolution in Russia in 1917. Another of the West's major concepts, democratic constitutionalism, appeared to have been tried in China after the 1911 revolution. In revolutionary eyes this had largely failed. Now was the time to turn to another theory, one that both explained why China had fallen behind the West and offered the way of recovering from that backwardness. The Marxist notion of imperialism, as developed by Lenin, defined the historical process by which capitalism imposed itself worldwide. The analysis seemed to fit the Chinese situation perfectly. China's victimisation by the imperialist powers was no mere accident; it was part of a dialectical pattern.

Yet it was precisely in that pattern that China's regeneration lay. The preordained triumph of the proletariat was the means by which China would throw off foreign domination and re-establish its traditional independence and greatness. At this stage, the lack of a proletariat in an orthodox sense was of no great importance. The essential aim of all Chinese revolutionaries was the restoration of China's past glories. However, it is important for the sake of balance to point out that the number of revolutionaries who embraced Marxism was relatively small. This made it correspondingly easier for the Comintern to target those revolutionaries likely to respond to Soviet approaches. Here again, the practical aspect was critical. The shrewd Bolshevik move in renouncing all claims to Chinese territory did much to convince radicals in China that Marxism in practice was a fulfilment of liberation theory.

2. China's place in Soviet Foreign Policy

Key question: Examine the role played by the Soviet Union in the formation of the CCP-GMD United Front.

In addition to reading section 2 of this chapter, it would be worthwhile consulting section 3b in Chapter 2.

Points to consider: The new Bolshevik government had been quick to make contact with the revolutionaries in China. The revolution of 1917 had failed to spread outside Russia; if the Bolsheviks could obtain support in the Far East it might go some way to compensate for the failure of the revolution to take hold in Europe. As Stalin claimed in the passage on page 118, China and Russia had much in common as victims of Western imperialism. Comintern agents had assisted in the creation of the CCP in July 1921. However, the critical fact about Bolshevik Russia and its Comintern agents was that in all things the Soviet Union came first. Chinese revolutionary aspirations were not judged on their own merits but only in relation to how they could be used to advance Russian interests. In regard to China, the Bolshevik government made the basic error of misreading the country's anti-colonialism as an expression of pro-Soviet sympathies. The Comintern rapidly came to the view that the Chinese Communist Party lacked the strength to be a truly revolutionary power on its own. The Comintern agents were more impressed with the GMD whose professed socialism they considered brought it into the Marxist camp. They also misread the situation in believing, wrongly, that the GMD was dominated not by the bourgeoisie but by pro-Soviet revolutionaries. They, therefore, urged the CCP to throw in its lot with the Nationalists. So, despite misgivings among some of its leading members, the CCP in 1922 accepted the Comintern instruction that it formally co-operate with the Guomindang.

3. The relations between Stalin and Mao Zedong

Key question: Consider the assertion that Stalin and Mao Zedong had fundamentally incompatible ideas concerning the character of the Chinese revolution.

Sections 3 to 7 of this chapter are required reading, but also see section 3d of Chapter 1, sections 3 and 4 of Chapter 2, and section 3 of chapter 3.

Points to consider: This question clearly calls for an examination of the personal contributions of the two leaders in question to Sino-Soviet relations. Despite Chiang's White Terror against the CCP in 1927, Stalin continued to assert that the GMD was working ultimately for a socialist revolution. Stalin's apparent blindness to the reality of the Chinese situation is explained by reference to the power struggle in the USSR. Stalin could not admit that Trotsky, in calling for the Soviet Union to change its policy and give total support to the CCP, had perceived the true situation in China. In condemning Trotsky, Stalin justified his pro-GMD, anti-CCP, stand by repeating the Comintern argument that in China's backward stage of the class war, the bourgeois Nationalists were the real revolutionaries and were to be supported, even at the expense of the Chinese Communists.

   Mao Zedong's experience of the United Front led him to the same conclusion as Trotsky - that Stalin and the Comintern were willing to sacrifice China's real interests. Mao was convinced that, since the Chinese were overwhelmingly a rural people, a genuine revolution could be achieved only through the peasantry. He had no compunction about altering Marxist-Leninist revolutionary theory to fit the Chinese context. From the 1920s onwards Mao rejected the priority of Stalin and the Comintern as interpreters of the character and needs of the Chinese revolution. In defiance of those Chinese Communists who accepted the party line dictated by the Soviet Union, Mao insisted that the Chinese would decide their own fate. In order to preserve the USSR's claim to leadership of world revolution Stalin was prepared to see the CCP destroyed; in order to save the CCP, and with it China's national struggle Mao Zedong was willing to restructure revolutionary theory in accordance with Chinese needs. Such conflicting attitudes left no common ground between the two leaders.

4. Sino-Soviet tensions, 1935-45

Key question: Why did the USSR remain reluctant to accord full recognition and support to the CCP until 1949?

Sections 4 to 6 of this chapter and sections 3, 5 and 6 of Chapter 3 are required reading.

Points to consider: The Long March and the creation of the Yanan Soviet owed nothing to Soviet assistance. Indeed, it was an act of defiance of Soviet orders. Had the CCP fully obeyed Comintern instructions it would not have left its besieged base in Jiangxi. Its new headquarters after 1935 in remote Yanan increased the CCP's sense of political as well as geographical remoteness from Stalin's Russia. Stalin believed that the Long March had been a defeat not a triumph for the Chinese Communists and he expected the remnants of the party that had reached Yanan to wither away. Gravely underestimating the strength of the CCP, the Soviet Union continued to give its support throughout the 1930s to Chiang Kaishek and his GMD government. Such news of the CCP at Yanan as reached Moscow seemed to confirm Stalin's conviction that Mao and his followers were renegade and heretical Marxists, 'white at heart' rather than committed 'red' revolutionaries.

Furthermore, it suited the USSR strategically to support the GMD since it was the Soviet belief that the Nationalist resistance to Japan after 1937 was the best means of deflecting Japanese ambitions away from Russia's Far Eastern borders. Involved in its massive struggle against Germany between 1941 and 1945, Stalin's Russia gave even less attention to the Chinese theatre. The dissolution of the Comintern in 1943 was a tacit acceptance by the USSR of its inability to influence Mao's Communists. Stalin's lack of faith in Mao and the CCP was further shown in August 1945 when the Soviet Union entered into a Treaty of Friendship with Chiang's GMD government. Even after the CCP-GMD civil war was resumed, following the defeat of Japan and it became evident just how powerful Mao's Communists had become in China, Stalin found it difficult to admit he had been wrong. The Kremlin continued to give its formal recognition to Chiang Kaishek as

China's legitimate leader. On the eve of Nationalists' withdrawal from the Chinese mainland, Stalin was still urging Mao's Communists to accept a north-south partition of China between themselves and the GMD. The triumph of the CCP in October 1949 was a fittingly ironic climax to a quarter of a century of Soviet failure to comprehend the Chinese situation.

5. The breakdown of Sino-Soviet relations

Key question: 'It was not revolutionary ideology but concern for national interests that divided China from the Soviet Union'. Discuss.

Sections 4 to 6 of this chapter and sections 3, 5 and 6 of Chapter 3 are required reading.

Points to consider: A critical consideration is that in China revolutionary theory was a means not an end. What all radicals, whether in the CCP or the GMD, wanted was Chinese regeneration, the reassertion of China's greatness. That is why Marxism appealed; it offered a programme for achieving that nationalist goal. In absorbing Marxism, the Chinese revolutionaries 'Sinified' it; they took from it those aspects that could best serve China's needs. At no point were the Chinese ready to forgo national interests for the sake of international revolution. That is why they were not prepared to accept dictation from the Soviet Union, which, it could be argued, was just as nationalistically minded as the Chinese. Despite the existence of the Comintern, Stalin's foreign policy was consistently orientated not to the furtherance of worldwide revolution but to the security and protection of the Soviet state. The 1917 Revolution in Russia was certainly an inspiration to the Chinese. However, what inspired them was not its proletarian but its anti-imperialist character. The Chinese revolutionaries were concerned less with fighting a class war than with engaging in an anti-colonialist struggle. Unable to grasp this, Stalin and the Comintern agents expected them to obey the instructions they were given. When the Chinese revolutionaries under Mao went their own way, their independence was condemned by Moscow as a betrayal of revolutionary principle. It was that fundamental divergence between the Soviet and Chinese readings of revolutionary duty that accounted for the increasing tension in Sino-Soviet relations in the period 1927-49.

Source analysis - *'China and the Soviet Union'*

The following is an analysis of a major document concerning Sino-Soviet relations that appears on page 127.

1 - Context

The Liberation Daily was the CCP's official newspaper published in

Yanan. As Mao Zedong's supremacy became more pronounced during the Yanan period, party publications tended to become a direct expression of his ideas and attitudes. Written in 1943, the piece is an uncritical report of a key speech given by Mao in response to the news that Stalin had recently ordered the dissolution of the Comintern.

2 - Meaning

The report records Mao's listing of the Comintern's major weaknesses. Effective leadership of national Communist parties required that the leaders be *in situ* and in constant touch with local conditions and developments; detached from the actual situation, the Comintern was no longer capable of providing such leadership. In what Mao referred to as 'the anti-Fascist struggle', meaning the Chinese resistance to Japan and the wider world war against the Axis powers, a rigid centralised Communist command structure lacked the flexibility to direct day-to-day policy. Moreover, such was the maturity of the separate national parties that they no longer needed the guidance of the Comintern. This was especially so in the case of China where the CCP had developed its own successful revolutionary tradition and anti-Japanese strategy without recourse to Comintern advice. To emphasise the CCP's independence, Mao stresses in a memorable phrase that revolution 'can be neither exported nor imported'. The Chinese revolution had been achieved by the Chinese proletariat. Mao's final flourish is to assert that true Marxism demands that once mere organisational bodies such as the Comintern have served their revolutionary purpose they 'should of course be abolished'.

3 - significance

Mao's observations are, in effect, a sustained justification for the independent line he had taken as a CCP leader since the mid-1920s. Stalin's acknowledgement that the Comintern was no longer an effective international revolutionary body gave validity to all that Mao had claimed and done during the Jiangxi and Yanan years. However, Stalin's abandonment of the Comintern had not been intended as an acceptance of the CCP's demands for independence. It was a decision taken at a stage in the Second World War when the Soviet Union, engaged in a desperate struggle with the occupying German forces, was anxious to impress its main ally, the USA, that it was no longer intent on fomenting anti-capitalist international revolution. Mao was aware of the international context; he had himself been willing for tactical reasons to soften the CCP's revolutionary social policies in order not to frighten off possible assistance from the Allied powers in the war against Japan. But his concern in the reported speech was to seize the opportunity offered by the dissolution of the Comintern to establish beyond doubt the right of the Chinese Communists to fashion their own revolution in their own way.

Since the 1920s when he and his followers had first defied Soviet instructions to remain in the United Front, Mao had been developing his own brand of Communism, free of Soviet influence. It differed markedly from the Soviet form in that it was a revolutionary movement based on the peasantry. Despite Mao's reference in his speech to the Chinese proletariat's role in creating the CCP, he was using the term proletariat in a sense opposite to that understood by Soviet Marxists. By proletariat they meant, as Marx and Lenin had, the industrial workers. Mao stood the term on its head; for him the proletariat were the peasantry. This fundamental difference of interpretation was forced on Mao by the plain fact that China did not have enough workers to form an industrial proletariat. If there was to be revolution in China it would have to be an affair of the peasants. In Soviet eyes Mao's cavalier re-ordering of the dialectic compounded his wilful refusal to conform to Moscow's orders regarding the revolutionary strategies to be followed in China. Mao's speech can be seen as a culmination of twenty years of increasing divergence between two increasingly incompatible forms of Marxism. His confident assertion that organisational forms should be jettisoned once they have outlived their usefulness clearly implied that the USSR, the world's first Marxist state, was becoming moribund. Such language presaged the bitter Sino-Soviet dispute that was to follow in the second half of the century over which of them had the moral right to the leadership of the international revolution.

CHAPTER 7

Conclusion

1 'A Revolution Against the World to Join the World'

China is a striking example of the problems that have afflicted those nations in the twentieth century that have tried to move from authoritarianism to democracy in one step. China's sense of its collective identity as a nation had been intimately bound up with its antique imperial system. When the empire collapsed there was no institution or ideology strong enough to take its place immediately. There followed a difficult period for China during which it tried to make Western concepts fill the void. Reformers and revolutionaries in China were faced with a dilemma. Instinctively, they rejected the West but they nevertheless appreciated that unless they copied Western ways they would not be able to modernise China in the form that they wished. This created a constant ambivalence in them, a tension between their feelings and their desires. Their feelings were a compound of hatred and distaste for the exploitation and acquisitiveness of the West; their desires were to emulate those foreign achievements that had given the West an undeniable superiority.

Since the opium wars of the 1840s, the Western imperialist powers had subordinated China to their own needs. This meant that any attempt on the part of the Chinese to assert their independence necessarily clashed with Western interests. All the reforming and revolutionary movements in China in the twentieth century started from the conviction that foreign influence had to be curtailed, if not removed entirely. Yet expulsion of the Westerners was achievable only by adopting Western ways. China of itself could not do it. Whether it was in the obvious area of military technology or in the less obvious, though equally important, matter of political ideology, China's salvation depended on its adoption of those aspects of Western culture that offered a chance of successful modernisation. At every step towards national consciousness, progressive Chinese were faced with the same paradox; the object of their bitterness, the West, was also the source of their inspiration. This is what gives particular validity to the definition of Chinese history in the twentieth century as 'a revolution against the world to join the world'.

The task of removing Western influence would never be easy for the reason that a significant number of Chinese had come to depend for their livelihood on the Western presence. This often compromised their nationalism. The dominant influence of the foreign concession areas in the major cities was a fact which none of the Chinese parties could afford to ignore. Western favours were not to be rejected out of hand simply on nationalist grounds. Western finance was necessary for Chinese regeneration. Depending on the character of their aims, the Chinese political parties had to do a range of deals with Western representatives. It was the GMD's need of capital that made Sun Yatsen, and to an even greater extent Chiang Kaishek, co-operate with the Western occupiers. Indeed, it is arguable that one basic reason why the GMD eventually lost the struggle with the CCP in 1949 was that it had proved too willing to accommodate itself to Western ways and values. This may have been done for expedient reasons but it left the impression that Chiang and the Nationalists were willing to settle for something less than complete Chinese independence.

It is noteworthy in this context that most of the GMD revolutionaries came from the Chinese littoral. Many had trained abroad: Japan was a natural attraction to them since there they could observe at first hand an Asian country moving successfully towards modernisation. The appeal of foreign ideas tended to detach them from the land and the mainstream of traditional Chinese culture. This may explain why the GMD lost touch with the mass of the Chinese people and why Mao Zedong and the Communists were able to adapt themselves so easily to Chinese history and make their revolution appear to grow naturally out of Chinese tradition. Mao chose to pursue a popular revolution by grounding it among the peasants who made up over four-fifths of the population. The leaders of the CCP may well have been middle-class intellectuals but the rank and file of the party were predominantly peasants of the hinterland. In contrast, the typical GMD member belonged to the urban class of eastern China. This explains in part why the GMD found it difficult to understand the needs or to serve the interests of the Chinese people as a whole.

2 Marxism-Leninism-Maoism and the Chinese Revolution

For Chinese revolutionaries, Communism had a double attraction; it provided both a programme for Chinese regeneration and a way of rejecting the West by embracing an ideology that the West found objectionable. Yet the Chinese absorption of Marxism was highly selective. As had traditionally happened with the other philosophies that it had incorporated, China took from Marxism those aspects which best suited the Chinese situation rather than forcing the Chinese situation to fit an overarching ideology. Marxism was to be the servant, not the master, of the Chinese revolution.

It is this subordination of Marxism to Chinese needs that explains the failure of Sino-Russian relations after 1917. Although the Bolshevik revolution was the great inspiration that led to the formation of the CCP, the Chinese revolutionaries never allowed the Bolshevik interpretation of the dialectic to direct the way they should conduct themselves. Stalin and his Comintern agents sent out a stream of instructions to the revolutionaries in China. Some members of the CCP faithfully adhered to these, but the most influential leaders of the party refused to follow the Russian path where they saw it conflicting with the interests of revolution as they perceived them. Mao Zedong is the outstanding example of this essentially pragmatic approach to the interpretation of Marxist principles. His frequent rejections of Russian approaches and ignoring of Comintern orders infuriated the Bolsheviks, but gave credibility to the emerging Marxist movement in China. Mao consistently maintained that had he followed Stalin's instructions the CCP would not have survived, let alone triumphed.

Mao Zedong did not follow a consistent programme of political action based upon predetermined theory. This is at its most evident in his interpretation of the way in which the dialectic operated within China. His experience as an organiser in the 1920s and 1930s, when he was struggling against the joint threat of Japan and the Guomindang, taught him that adherence to pure theory would be suicidal. He came to believe that proletarian revolution based upon the urban areas was unachievable in China. If there was to be revolution it would have to come from the Chinese people, 80 per cent of whom were peasants. This offended orthodox Marxist theorists, who argued that the role and the duty of revolutionaries was to conform to the scientific laws of the dialectic, whose stages could not be jumped at will. But, as Trotsky perceived, Mao's interpretation was the only one having practical validity in the Chinese context. Mao considered that the rate of urban growth was far too slow for an industrially based proletarian rising to occur; for China, therefore, a rising of the peasants would be sufficient to fulfil the dialectical imperative.

It is not the depth, but the popularity of Mao's ideas that is most impressive. Indeed, it is their apparent simplicity that is so striking. He provided the peasants with an easily understandable set of guidelines which, when followed, gave them for the first time a degree of control over their own fate. This sensitivity towards the ordinary people was in marked contrast, not only to the harsh methods of the Guomindang, but also to the mixture of indifference and contempt with which Westerners had traditionally treated the Chinese. It is not an exaggeration to say that the pro-peasant policy of Mao's Red Army introduced into China a hitherto unapplied, if not unknown, humanitarian concept. Mao's name and that of his troops, became a byword among the peasants for sympathy and compassion.

Doubts still remain for the historian, however. Communist legend has it that Yanan was a time of creativity and harmony when Mao as the unchallenged leader of the CCP made his party one with the Chinese people. That picture we now know to be a distortion. The story is still not wholly clear but there is considerable evidence that Mao was involved in a desperate power struggle within the party for much of that time. The affection of some of the people for the Red Army may have been whole-hearted but when the Communists felt their interests to be under threat they were as capable as their GMD opponents of behaving ruthlessly in the localities they controlled.

Yet Mao through his sense of political realism had perceived what would best appeal to an oppressed population. By virtue of his organising ability and awesome power to inspire others, Mao won the loyalty of a large part of the population in the face of what often appeared to be impossible odds. He may have employed unscrupulous methods, as at Futien, to impose himself on the party and the party on the localities, but his dedication to the Chinese people was beyond question. It is arguable that without 'the helmsman' Communism would not have survived in China, leave alone prove triumphant in 1949. Not only did Mao win a civil war; he established the independent existence of an alternative form of communism, an achievement of momentous consequences in the international history of the twentieth century.

3 Sino-Western Misunderstanding

Two particular and connected features dominate the modern history of China's relations with the West: the consistent policy of the Western powers to use China for their own ends accompanied by an unwillingness on their part to understand the real character of China. Indeed, there seemed to exist a mutual incomprehension between the two cultures. Looking back upon Sino-Western relations in this period it is remarkable how little the West really knew about China. Westerners had for so long been intent on the economic or strategic exploitation of China that they had given themselves little opportunity to understand the culture or politics of the Chinese. Few of the expatriates who lived there made a genuine attempt to adopt Chinese ways or integrate themselves into Chinese culture. Real China experts were rarities. China was a large and confusing country; the information which came out seldom gave a complete picture of what was going on. Western ignorance was especially notable in regard to China's internal politics. Consumed with their own economic and diplomatic concerns, neither Europe nor the USA fully grasped the nature or significance of the divisions between the Nationalists and the Communists. After the withdrawal of Mao and the CCP to Yanan in 1936, Western observers tended to assume that the Communists were a spent force. Minimal diplomatic contact was made between Mao and the West during the Yanan period.

The result was that, however weak Chiang's Nationalist government may have been, it was convenient for the West to regard it as legitimately representing the Chinese nation. With the development of the European war into a world war in 1941, China came to be numbered as one of the Allies and was accorded world status. This was an extraordinary situation; Chiang Kaishek was recognised as leader of the nation and an international statesman at the very time he and the GMD were being overtaken in strength and popularity by Mao Zedong and the CCP.

What complicated the issue was that after 1936 the two warring Chinese factions ostensibly formed a united front against Japan. This is what made it so difficult for the Western world to understand the true situation in China. Preoccupied as they were with the world war in its wider aspects, the powers tended to see China in the simplest terms. Since Chiang Kaishek was acknowledged, even by the CCP after the Xian Incident in 1936, as the leader of the Front, it was natural that the USA and her wartime allies should regard dealing directly with him as the most logical position to adopt in their combined struggle against Japan. After 1949 Mao would bitterly criticise the USA and its allies for continuing to support Chiang Kaishek and the Nationalists, but here he was being disingenuous. It is arguable that many Chinese themselves did not understand the politics of their land. How much more difficult then for the outsider to differentiate between the rival claimants. What appears clear to later analysts was often opaque to contemporaries. At the time, what foreign observers perceived was a China desperate to throw off the Japanese yoke, with its two main parties, which were themselves coalitions of interests, acting together in a common endeavour.

This, of course, was not the case. The truth was that Chiang throughout had as his priority the crushing of the Reds, while the CCP joined forces with the Nationalists for essentially expedient reasons. Mao's collaboration with the GMD government had always been conditional and strategic; given their ideology and determination to take power in China, it is unthinkable that Mao's Communists would give lasting recognition to the legitimacy of the Guomindang regime. Consequently, the term United Front was a misnomer. However, it would have required a very astute surveyor of the Chinese situation to appreciate these distinctions. After all, there was constant rivalry, not merely between, but also within, the major parties. Furthermore, the many regional differences in a country as vast as China could not easily be represented by one single party or set of parties. The numerous breakaway groups and would-be leaders who litter the history of these years testify to that. Given these factors, it would be unbalanced to criticise the West too strongly for its misreading of the Chinese political situation.

Arguably, America's greatest failing was not, as Mao would have it, its imperialism towards China, but its ignorance of Chinese politics. The Cold War debate would subsequently turn in hindsight all America's actions post-1917 into pieces played on the great international chess board. But that is to impose a pattern on events that did not necessarily apply at the time. It may have been misguided, but America's policy towards China was genuine. Certainly the USA's initial concern was not to enforce a particular political settlement on China. That came later when it was obliged to take sides in the 1945-9 Nationalist-Communist struggle. The USA's persistence in supporting Chiang and the Nationalists long after they had been shown to have lost 'the hearts of the people' is a part of that basic failure of understanding that for so long had distorted China's relations with the outside world.

That both the USA and the USSR had failed to recognise the true character of the Chinese revolutionary movement increased China's sense of isolation. It was thrown back on to its age-old conviction that all influences from outside were inimical to its interests. The results were of immense significance: China's revolution defined itself as an essentially anti-foreigner movement, anti-Soviet as well as anti-Western. China increasingly believed that its salvation could come only from within. Under Mao Zedong after 1949 this would become more than simply a reassertion of China's traditional independence. It became a form of national paranoia in which the Chinese People's Republic saw itself as standing alone in a hostile world that was bent on China's destruction.

Using the 'Conclusion'

This chapter advances three main propositions:

1. The significance of Chinese history in the period 1900-49 is best understood as 'a revolution against the world to join the world', the implication being that China was involved in a paradox - attempting to achieve political and economic modernisation by adopting the progressive features of the Western world whose previous exploitation of China was the present cause of the nation's relative backwardness.

2. Superficially the victory of the CCP over the GMD in 1949 was a triumph of international Marxism-Leninism. But in reality it was the assertion of a particularly intense form of Chinese nationalism. In developing his own brand of revolution Mao had broken from Moscow, defied the Comintern, and established an independent form of Communism.

3. The traditional pattern of contact between China and the West, that of exploited and exploiter, created a legacy of mutual suspicion and misunderstanding that vitiated subsequent Sino-Western relations. The result was that by 1949 the successful Chinese revolutionaries saw themselves as beleaguered in a world that was essentially hostile.

The student should test these arguments by referring to the relevant chapters in this book and by comparing them with the ideas contained in the texts listed in the further reading section.

Chronological Table

1895	Defeat of China by Japan
1895-9	Western 'scramble for concessions' in China
1898	The 100 Days' reforms
1898	Britain acquired 99-year lease on Kowloon
1889	USA declared its 'open door' policy
1900	Boxer risings
	Emperor Guangxu and Dowager Empress Cixi fled to Xian
1902	Guangxu and Cixi returned to Beijing
	Anglo-Japanese Alliance
1904	British demanded recognition of Tibetan independence
1904-5	Russo-Japanese War
1905	Russia recognised Japan's special influence in Manchuria
	Republican Party set up
	Chinese boycott of American goods
	Alliance League founded
1908	Death of Dowager Empress Cixi
	Root-Takahira agreement between USA and Japan
1909	Yuan Shikai dismissed
	President Taft urged China to accept increased US investment
1910	Korea annexed by Japan
1911	Double Tenth Rising at Wuhan
	Nanjing declared for a Chinese republic
	International Banking Commission established
1912	Sun Yatsen installed as President of the Republic
	Yuan Shikai took over from Sun as President
	Manchu abdication
	Republic set up
	Guomindang formed
	Yuan Shikai refused to recognise Nanjing government
1913	'Second Revolution' failed
	Parliament suspended
	GMD proscribed
	Sun Yatsen fled to Japan
1914	Outbreak of war in Europe
1915	Japan's 21 Demands

1916	Yuan Shikai enthroned as Emperor
	Death of Yuan Shikai
1916-26	Era of the warlords
1917	Attempt to restore Manchus failed
	China declared war on Germany
	October Revolution in Russia
1918	Sino-Japanese military alliance signed
	End of war in Europe
1918-20	Russian Civil War
1919	Versailles Settlement humiliated China
	4 May Movement began
1921	Comintern agents visited China
	CCP created
1921-2	Washington Conference
	Comintern sent Joffe and Borodin to China
	GMD friendship pact with Moscow
	CCP Congress voted for union with GMD
1924	CCP-GMD United Front formed
	Russia seized Outer Mongolia
	GMD constitution published
1925	Death of Sun Yatsen
	30 May Incident
	Chiang Kaishek became leader of GMD
1926-8	Northern Expedition
1927	Chiang's 'White Terror' unleashed
	Failure of Autumn Harvest. Rising led by Mao Zedong
	Nationalist Government established at Nanjing
	Tanaka Memorial
1927-34	Jiangxi period
1931	Mukden incident
	Japanese occupation of Manchuria
1932	Creation of Manchukuo with Pu Yi installed as Emperor
1933	Withdrawal of Japan from the League of Nations
1934-5	Long March
1935	Mao defeated the urban Reds in the critical CCP vote at Zunyi
1935-45	Yanan period
1936	Xian Incident
	Germany and Japan signed the Anti-Comintern Pact

1937-45	Sino-Japanese War
1937	Second CCP-GMD United Front
	Beijing, Shanghai and Nanjing fell to Japan
	Rape of Nanjing
1938	Nationalist capital moved from Nanjing to Chongqing
1939	Nazi-Soviet Pact signed
1940-4	'New Government of China' led by Wang Jingwei at Nanjing
1940	Mao Zedong's *On New Democracy* published
	USA attempted to impose international oil ban on Japan
1941	Non-aggression pact signed between USSR and Japan
	Japan's attack on Pearl Harbor
1942	Britain and USA abandoned extraterritoriality in China
1943	Chiang Kaishek's *China's Destiny* published
	Dissolution of Comintern
	Chiang Kaishek attended Cairo Conference
	Mao Zedong's 'Rectification of Conduct Campaign' introduced
1944	Mao Zedong proposed CCP-GMD coalition
	General Stilwell recalled from China
1945	Mao-Chiang discussions
	Chiang rejected notion of sharing power with CCP
	Yalta Conference
	Death of President Roosevelt
	Truman became President
	Atomic bombing of Hiroshima and Nagasaki
	USSR declared war on Japan
	USSR occupied Manchuria
	Japanese surrender
	Sino-Soviet Treaty of Friendship
	General Marshall sent as special US envoy to China
1945-9	CCP-GMD civil war
1948	GMD atrocities in Shanghai
	Nationalists defeated at Mukden
	Communist victory at Hsuchow
1949	Nationalists surrendered Beijing to the Communists
	Nanjing, Shanghai, and Guangzhou fell to the Red Army

Further Reading

The following is a very selective list of the many studies of late imperial and republican China, written in English or now available in English translation. Where possible, reference is to the latest paperback edition.

1 General Surveys

The outstanding reference book on the period is *The Cambridge History of China*, edited by **D. Twitchett** and **J. Fairbank.** The relevant volumes are numbers 11-13, Imperial and Republican China (CUP 1982-6). These can be heavy going in places but among the contributors are some of the chief authorities on modern Chinese history, including many of the writers below.

A lively and comprehensive overview of modern China is to be found in **Dick Wilson,** *China: the Big Tiger* (Little Brown, 1996) and in **John Gittings,** *Real China: from Cannibalism to Karaoke* (Simon & Schuster, 1996). A major work by a leading analyst of Chinese history is **James E. Sheridan's** *China in Disintegration 1912-49,* (The Free Press, Macmillan, 1975). A particularly clear treatment is in **Richard C. Thornton**'s *China: a Political History 1917-80* (Westview Press, 1982) while an interesting perspective is provided by the Hong-Kong Chinese historian, **W.S.K. Waung,** in his *Revolution and Liberation: A Short History of Modern China 1900-1970* (Heinemann, 1971). A very useful short introduction, containing a full list of modern works, is **P.J.Bailey's** *China in the Twentieth Century* (Basil Blackwell, 1988). Other broad surveys of particular value are **S.A.M. Adshead,** *China in World History* (Macmillan, 1995) and **John King Fairbank,** *China: A New History* (Belknap Press, 1992); the latter has an excellent bibliography. Also to be recommended are **Henry McAleavy,** *The Modern History of China* (Weidenfeld and Nicholson, 1967), written by a British scholar who lived in China in the 1930s and 1940s, and **Peter M. Mitchell,** *China: Tradition and Revolution* (Edward Arnold, 1977), which puts the revolutionary developments in China in their historical perspective.

A work which seeks to describe the history of the period from the point of view of lesser-known figures in Chinese public life is **Jonathan Spence's** *The Gate of Heavenly Peace: the Chinese and their Revolution 1895-1980* (Faber and Faber ,1982). Another key analysis by **Spence** is his *The Search for Modern China* (W.W. Norton, 1990). An important example of French Marxist scholarship, containing detailed maps and sets of primary sources, is **Jean Chesneaux, Francoise Le Barbier** and **Marie-Claire Bergere,** *China from the 1911 Revolution to Liberation* (Harvester Press,1980). An especially interesting analysis of the period from a Chinese non-Maoist angle is **Li Chien-Nung's** *The*

Political History of China (Van Nostrand, 1956).
Immanuel C.Y. Hsu in *The Rise of Modern China,* (New York, 1983) deals with the political struggles of the period. The author also edited an interesting set of interpretations under the title *Readings in Modern Chinese History* (Oxford, 1971). **Dun J. Li,** *The Road to Communism: China Since 1912* (Van Nostrand, 1969) contains a wide range of illuminating sources. **F. Schurmann** and **O. Schell** have edited two books of useful source material: *Imperial China* (Penguin, 1968) and *Republican China* (Penguin, 1974).

2 Particular themes

Frederic Wakeman, *The Fall of Imperial China* (New York, 1975) is an absorbing account of the fall of the Qing dynasty. The same can be said of **Christopher Hibbert's** racier *The Dragon Wakes: China 1795-1911* (Longmans, 1970).

Of the vast number of works on the Boxer rising **Joseph Esherick's** *The Origins of the Boxer Uprising* (University of California Press, 1987) is one of the most readable.

An important collection of essays on China's economic relations with the West is contained in *China's Modern Economy in Historical Perspective* edited by **Dwight Perkins** (Stanford University Press, 1975).

An interesting collaboration between Japanese and American scholars produced *The 1911 Revolution: Interpretive Essays,* edited by **Shinkichi Eto** and **Harold Schiffrin** (University of Tokyo Press, 1984).

The place of ideology in the growth of Chinese nationalism is covered in **Chow Tse-tung,** *The May Fourth Movement: Intellectual Revolution in Modern China* (Harvard University Press, 1960) and in **Vera Schwartz,** *The Chinese Enlightenment: Intellectuals and the Legacy of the May Fourth Movement of 1919* (University of California Press, 1986).

A work dealing with Sino-Soviet relations in the 1920s is **Michael Y.L. Luk,** *The Origins of Chinese Bolshevism: An Ideology in the Making, 1920-28* (Oxford University Press, 1989).

The warlord period is covered in **Hsi-shenh Ch'i,** *Warlord Politics in China, 1916-1928* (Stanford University Press, 1976).

Edgar Snow, an American supporter of Mao who lived for some time with the Communists, wrote two eye-witness accounts of particular interest: *Red Star Over China,* (Penguin, 1951) and *The Long March* (Penguin, 1973). An informed later study of the Long March is **Benjamin Young's** *From Revolution to Politics: Chinese Communists on the Long March* (Westview Press, 1990). Similar to Edgar Snow in approach is **William Hinton.** In 1948 he recorded at first hand the Communist takeover of a rural area. His approving account is contained in his *Fanshen: A Documentary study of Revolution in a Chinese Village* (Penguin, 1972).

Lloyd Eastman has edited a largely critical view of the Guomindang period, *The Nationalist Era in China, 1927-37* (Cambridge University Press, 1991). A more sympathetic picture is drawn in **Hung-mao Tien's** *Government and Politics in Kuomintang China, 1927-49* (Stanford University Press, 1972).

An absorbing view of Chinese history is provided by the anti-Stalinist but pro-Soviet Russian writer, **Roy Medvedev** in the early chapters of his *China and the Superpowers* (Blackwell, 1986). **Wang Ming's** *Mao Tse-tung* (Moscow, 1975) is a rare example of a pro-Soviet, anti-Maoist Chinese writer.

A book which illustrates a range of Japanese views on the China question is **James W. Morley,** ed., *The China Quagmire: Japan's Expansion on the Asian Continent, 1933-41, Selected Translations* (Columbia University Press, 1983).

CCP-GMD relations during the war against Japan are fully described in **Kui-kwong Shum,** *The Chinese Communists' Road to Power: The Anti-Japanese National United Front, 1939-1945* (Oxford University Press, 1988). An important work dealing with Sino-Western relations in that same period is **Christopher Thorne,** *Allies of a Kind: The United States, Britain and the War against Japan 1941-1945* (Oxford University Press 1988)

The final struggle between the Guomindang and the Communists is described in **Suzanne Pepper,** *Civil War in China: The Political Struggle, 1945-1949* (University of California Press, 1978).

3 Biographies

A recommended study of 'the father of the Chinese Republic' is **M. Wibur's** *Sun Yat-sen: Frustrated Patriot* (New York, 1976).

The best study of China's first republican president is **Jerome Ch'en's,** *Yuan Shi-Kai, 1859-1916* (Stanford University Press ,1972). Also useful is **E. Young's** *The Presidency of Yuan Shih-k'ai* (Ann Arbor, 1977).

Lee Feigon's, *Chen Duxiu, the Founder of the CCP* (Princeton, 1983) deals with an important Chinese Communist who had a major influence on Mao Zedong.

A book which paints the GMD leader in as favourable light as possible is **Emily Hahn's** *Chiang Kai-shek, an Unauthorised Biography* (New York, 1955). **Louise Strong's** *China Fights for Freedom* (New World Press, 1963) is a less sympathetic study of Chiang and the Nationalists in their struggle against the Japanese; **S. Hsiung's** *The Life of Chiang Kai-Shek* (Peter Davies, 1948), is a book which, since Hsiung was a close friend of Chiang, gives an insider's account of the the power struggle within the GMD. For a strongly critical account of the inefficiency and corruption of Chiang's regime consult **T.H. White** and **A. Jacoby,** *Thunder Out of China* (London, 1951). It is worth comparing and contrasting these works with the Japanese viewpoint as expressed in **Keiji Furuya's** *Chiang Kai-shek: His Life and Times* (St.John's University, 1981).

An authoritative biography of the CCP leader is **Stuart Schram's** *Mao Tse-Tung* (Penguin, 1975). Also valuable is the same author's *Mao Tse-Tung Unrehearsed, Talks and letters: 1956-71* (Penguin, 1975). Although it relates mainly to Mao's career after 1949, it does contain interesting references to the earlier years. Another highly regarded study is **Jerome Ch'en's** *Mao and the Chinese Revolution* (Oxford University Press ,1965). An idiosyncratic but highly readable treatment of Mao is by the American traveller and journalist, **Harrison E. Salisbury,** *The New Emperors Mao and Deng: A Dual Biography,* (HarperCollins, 1993). A particularly notable biography, based on the recollections of one of Mao's bodyguards, is **Quan Yanchi's** *Mao Zedong: Man Not God* (Foreign Languages Press, Beijing 1992). As its title suggests, it offers a balanced appraisal, something unknown in China before the 1980s when only hagiography was permitted. Among those books which adopt a strongly critical stance towards the role of Mao and the CCP in republican China are **Siao Yu's** *Mao and I Were Beggars* (Syracuse University, 1959).

Extracts from Mao Zedong's major works, accompanied by an informed introduction to his career are to be found in **Ann Freemantle,** *Mao Tse-tung: An Anthology of his Writings,* (Mentor, 1971). The student is encouraged at least to glance at *Quotations from Chairman Mao Tse-Tung* (Foreign Languages Press, Peking, 1966); popularly known as 'the little Red Book' which became the bible of China in the 1960s.

The earlier chapters of **David Goodman's** *Deng Xiaoping* (Cardinal, 1990) throw an interesting light on the CCP's internal struggles pre-1949.

Glossary

Glossary of Chinese names in their Pinyin and Wade Giles forms

Pinyin	Wade-Giles	Pinyin	Wade-Giles
Anhui	Anhwei	Nanjing	Nanking
Beijing	Peking	Qingdao	Tsingtao
Chen Duxui	Chen Tu-hsiu	Shaanxi	Shensi
Chongqing	Chungking	Shandong	Shantung
Cixi	Tsu-hsi	Shanxi	Shansi
Deng Xiaoping	Teng Hsiao-ping	Sun Yatsen	Sun Yat-sen
		Sichuan	Szechwan
Duan Qirui	Tuan Chi-jui	Taiwan	Formosa
Feng Yuxiang	Feng Yu-hsiang	Wang Jingwei	Wang Ching-wei
Fuzhou	Foochow	Wuhan	Wuchang
Fujian	Fukien	Xian	Sian
Gansu	Kansu	Xinjiang	Sinkiang
Guangzhou	Canton	Yanan	Yenan
Guandong	Kwangtung	Yangzi	Yangtze
Guangxu	Kuang Hsu	Yan Xishan	Yen Hsi-shan
Guizhou	Kweichow	Yuan Shikai	Yuan Shi-kai
Guomindang	Kuomintang	Zhang Guotao	Chang Kuo-tao
Henan	Honan	Zhang Xun	Chang Xun
Hubei	Hupei	Zhang Xue-liang	Chang Hsueh-liang
Jiang Jieshi	Chiang Kai-shek	Zhang Zuolin	Chang Tso-lin
Jiang Qing	Chiang Ching	Zhang Zongzhang	Chang Tsung-chang
Jiangxi	Kiansi		
Lin Biao	Lin Piao	Zhejiang	Chekiang
Liu Shaoqi	Liu Shao-chi	Zhou Enlai	Chou En-lai
Li Dazhao	Li Ta-chao,	Zhu De	Chuh Teh
Mao Zedong	Mao Tse-tung	Zunyi	Tsunyi
Mukden	Shenyang		

Index